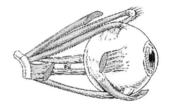

DK BACKPACK BOOKS

1,001 FACTS ABOUT
THE HUMAN BODY

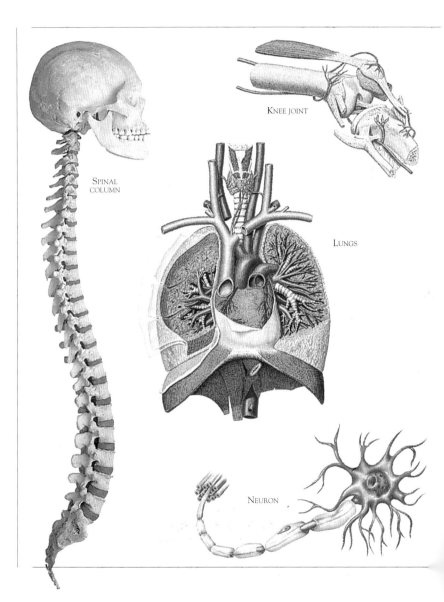

KNEE JOINT

SPINAL COLUMN

LUNGS

NEURON

BACKPACK BOOKS

1,001 FACTS ABOUT THE HUMAN BODY

Written by
DR SARAH BREWER

Additional material by
DR NAOMI CRAFT

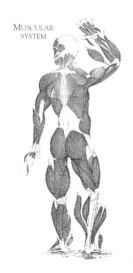

MUSCULAR
SYSTEM

SKULL

LYMPHATIC
SYSTEM

DORLING KINDERSLEY
London • New York • Stuttgart

LONDON, NEW YORK, MUNICH
MELBOURNE, DELHI

Editor Simon Mugford
Designer Dan Green
Senior editor Andrew Macintyre
Design manager Jane Thomas
DTP designer Jill Bunyan
Production Nicola Torode
With thanks to the original team
Project editor Caroline Brooke
Designer Kate Eagar
Picture research Sarah Crouch
Production Josie Alabaster

First published in Great Britain in 2002
by Dorling Kindersley Limited
80 Strand, London WC2R 0RL
A Penguin company

A CIP catalogue record for this book is available from
the British Library

ISBN 0 7513 4416 8

Colour reproduction by Colourscan
Printed and bound in Singapore

See our complete catalogue at
www.dk.com

CONTENTS

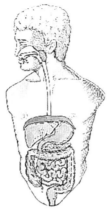

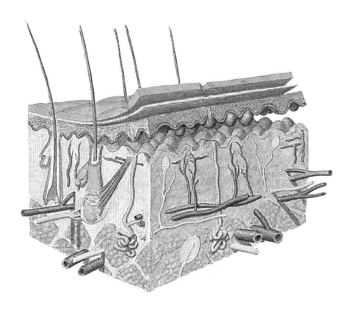

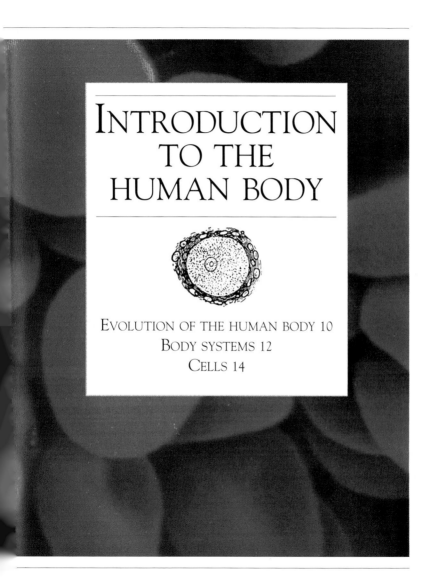

INTRODUCTION TO THE HUMAN BODY

EVOLUTION OF THE HUMAN BODY

LIFE ON EARTH probably began four billion years ago. Single-celled organisms gradually evolved into more complex multicelled plants and animals. Fossils suggest that humanlike creatures, hominids, first appeared five million years ago.

TIME-SCALE OF EARTH'S EXISTENCE

Earth formed 4.6 billion years ago

Bacteria

Humans

Apes

Dinosaurs

Land plants

Marine life 1.5 billion years ago

3.8 billion years ago

EVOLUTIONARY CLOCK
Human life is a relatively recent occurrence in the history of life on Earth.

Sivapithecus
c.7–13 million years ago. Extinct ancestor of the orang-utan

Orang-utan
Skull of modern monkey shows that orangutans belong to a different mammal family than either humans or apes

Chimpanzee/gorilla
Modern apes walk on all fours and have smaller brains than humans

Australopithecus
1.5–5 million years ago. Early ape-people may have been the first to walk upright

HUMAN FAMILY TREE

Aegyptopithecus
30 million years ago. Earliest known ancestor of apes and

PROCESS

Hominids are thought to have originated in East Africa and to have been closely related to the great ape. Hominids began to lose body hair, walk upright on two feet, and use their hands to perform more complex tasks. Their brain became larger as their language and reasoning powers developed.

Homo habilis
1.5–2 million years ago.
A hunter-scavenger who had a basic form of speech

Homo erectus
0.5–1.5 million years ago.
More skillful people who lived in huts, they could produce a variety of sounds and make fire

Performed burial ceremonies and wore animal skins

Homo sapiens neanderthalensis
30,000–200,000 years ago.
Neanderthals had overhanging brows, large noses, and undeveloped chins

Homo sapiens sapiens
40,000 years ago.
Modern humans populated many parts of the world; they wore more refined clothes and produced art

Heavy features

SKULL OF HOMO SAPIENS NEANDERTHALENSIS

Fine features

SKULL OF HOMO SAPIENS SAPIENS

SKULLS

Fossil skulls provide the best evidence of evolution. Differences in the structure of the brow, nose, jaws, and teeth help to identify which hominid species the skull belongs to.

EVOLUTION FACTS

• About two million years ago, there were several species of hominids living at the same time.

• *Homo sapiens sapiens* is the only existing species of hominid.

• The earliest hominid fossils are from about 3.5 million years ago.

11

BODY SYSTEMS

THE HUMAN BODY IS made up of a number of systems. Each one performs a particular function. All the systems are linked together and communicate through the blood and nervous system. Here are the major systems of the body common to both sexes.

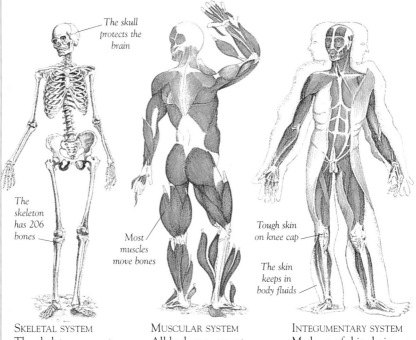

The skull protects the brain

The skeleton has 206 bones

Most muscles move bones

Tough skin on knee cap

The skin keeps in body fluids

SKELETAL SYSTEM
The skeleton supports the body and protects the internal organs, such as the heart and lungs.

MUSCULAR SYSTEM
All body movement (involuntary and voluntary) is due to the contraction of muscles.

INTEGUMENTARY SYSTEM
Made up of skin, hair, and nails, this system protects the body and keeps it waterproof.

RESPIRATORY SYSTEM
This system draws oxygenated air into the lungs and pushes out waste gases.

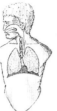

DIGESTIVE SYSTEM
The 9m (28 ft)-long digestive tract digests food and eliminates solid body wastes.

URINARY SYSTEM
Soluble wastes and fluids are filtered from the blood for disposal as urine.

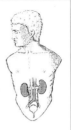

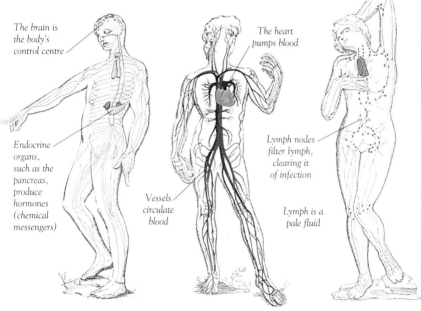

The brain is the body's control centre

The heart pumps blood

Endocrine organs, such as the pancreas, produce hormones (chemical messengers)

Vessels circulate blood

Lymph nodes filter lymph, clearing it of infection

Lymph is a pale fluid

NERVOUS SYSTEM
This sends nerve signals to and from the brain. The endocrine system carries hormonal messages.

CARDIOVASCULAR SYSTEM
Pumping blood around the body, this system provides tissues with oxygen and removes waste products.

LYMPHATIC SYSTEM
Lymph, containing immune cells, is collected by a network of lymph vessels.

13

CELLS

BODY SYSTEMS are made up of organs containing different tissues. A tissue is a collection of similar cells that perform a specific function. Over 200 types of specialized cell act as the body's building blocks.

CELL FEATURES
Cells contain structures called organelles ("little organs"), which carry out many vital functions. Cells are bathed in fluid, which brings them oxygen and nutrients. It also takes away products, such as hormones, and wastes, such as carbon dioxide.

CELL FACTS

• The adult human body contains over 50 trillion cells.

• Three billion of the body's cells die every minute; most are renewed.

• An egg cell (ovum) is the largest human cell. It can just be seen without a microscope.

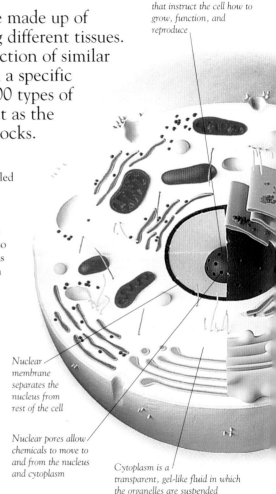

Nucleus contains genes (units of inherited material) that instruct the cell how to grow, function, and reproduce

Nuclear membrane separates the nucleus from rest of the cell

Nuclear pores allow chemicals to move to and from the nucleus and cytoplasm

Cytoplasm is a transparent, gel-like fluid in which the organelles are suspended

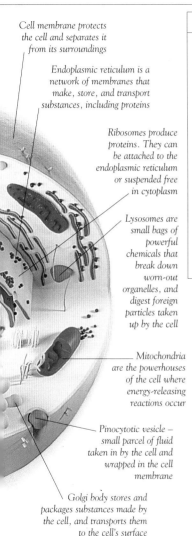

Cell membrane protects the cell and separates it from its surroundings

Endoplasmic reticulum is a network of membranes that make, store, and transport substances, including proteins

Ribosomes produce proteins. They can be attached to the endoplasmic reticulum or suspended free in cytoplasm

Lysosomes are small bags of powerful chemicals that break down worn-out organelles, and digest foreign particles taken up by the cell

Mitochondria are the powerhouses of the cell where energy-releasing reactions occur

Pinocytotic vesicle – small parcel of fluid taken in by the cell and wrapped in the cell membrane

Golgi body stores and packages substances made by the cell, and transports them to the cell's surface

TYPES OF CELL

RED BLOOD CELLS
The only cells to lack a nucleus, these cells carry oxygen and live for about 120 days.

NERVE CELLS
These are the longest cells in the body. Nerve cells transport electrical messages.

WHITE BLOOD CELLS
About 10 billion new white blood cells are made every day. They help fight infection.

Nucleus

NUCLEUS STARTS TO GROW

NUCLEUS STARTS TO DIVIDE

FIRST NUCLEUS, THEN CELL, DIVIDES IN TWO

EACH CELL MAY GROW TO SIZE OF PARENT CELL

CELL DIVISION
Cells divide and multiply to allow us to grow. They divide at the fastest rate during a baby's development in the womb. In later life, when growth has stopped, cells divide at a slower rate, to replace worn-out cells.

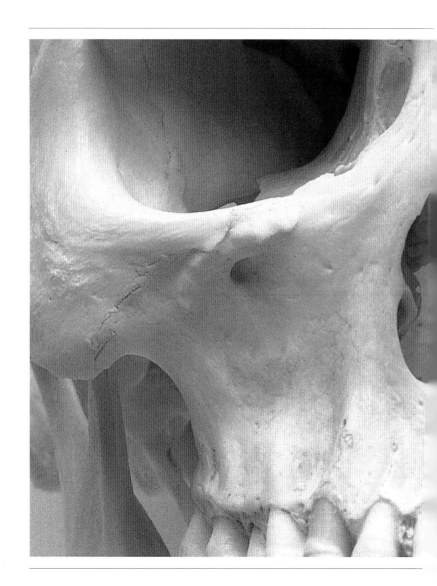

BODY STRUCTURES

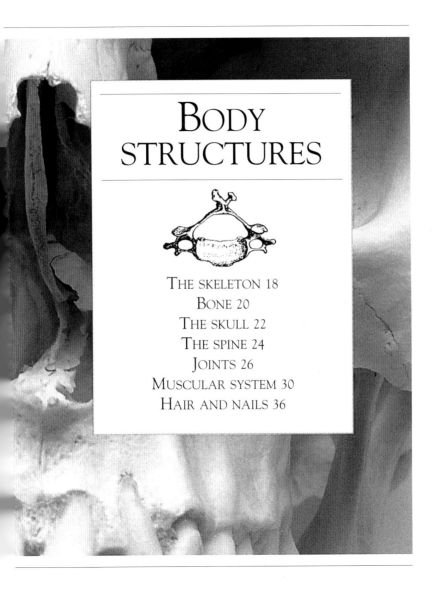

THE SKELETON

THE BODY'S FRAMEWORK is the skeleton. It provides shape and protection, and acts as an anchor for muscles to allow the body to move. Made up of hard bones and softer cartilage, the skeleton is a living tissue, and is constantly being renewed. Females usually have smaller, lighter skeletons than males.

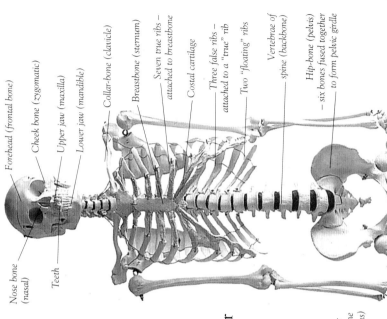

Forehead (frontal bone)

Cheek bone (zygomatic)

Upper jaw (maxilla)

Lower jaw (mandible)

Collar-bone (clavicle)

Breastbone (sternum)

Seven true ribs – attached to breastbone

Costal cartilage

Three false ribs – attached to a "true" rib

Two "floating" ribs

Vertebrae of spine (backbone)

Hip-bone (pelvis) – six bones fused together to form pelvic girdle

Nose bone (nasal)

Teeth

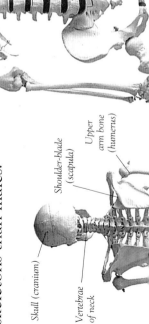

Skull (cranium)

Vertebrae of neck

Shoulder-blade (scapula)

Upper arm bone (humerus)

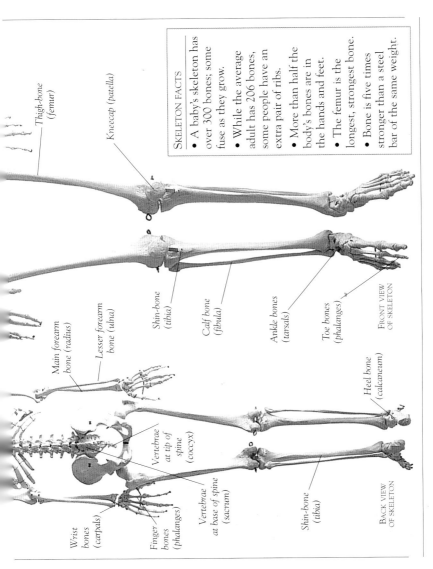

Thigh-bone (*femur*)

Kneecap (*patella*)

SKELETON FACTS

- A baby's skeleton has over 300 bones; some fuse as they grow.

- While the average adult has 206 bones, some people have an extra pair of ribs.

- More than half the body's bones are in the hands and feet.

- The femur is the longest, strongest bone.

- Bone is five times stronger than a steel bar of the same weight.

Main forearm bone (*radius*)

Lesser forearm bone (*ulna*)

Shin-bone (*tibia*)

Calf bone (*fibula*)

Ankle bones (*tarsals*)

Toe bones (*phalanges*)

FRONT VIEW OF SKELETON

Vertebrae at tip of spine (*coccyx*)

Heel bone (*calcaneum*)

Wrist bones (*carpals*)

Finger bones (*phalanges*)

Vertebrae at base of spine (*sacrum*)

Shin-bone (*tibia*)

BACK VIEW OF SKELETON

BONE

MADE UP OF A NETWORK of protein fibres (collagen) filled with calcium and phosphate, bone is strong and alive. It is constantly remodelling itself, with ten per cent of its mass being replaced each year. This process involves some cells (osteoclasts) breaking down old bone, while other cells (osteoblasts) build up new bone.

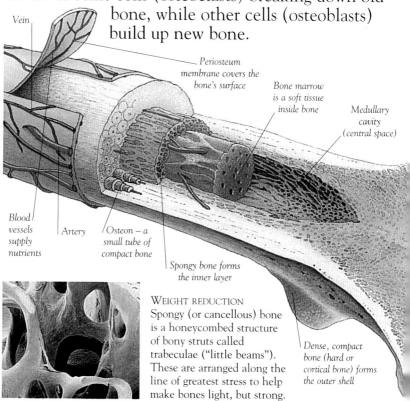

Vein

Periosteum membrane covers the bone's surface

Bone marrow is a soft tissue inside bone

Medullary cavity (central space)

Blood vessels supply nutrients

Artery

Osteon – a small tube of compact bone

Spongy bone forms the inner layer

Dense, compact bone (hard or cortical bone) forms the outer shell

WEIGHT REDUCTION
Spongy (or cancellous) bone is a honeycombed structure of bony struts called trabeculae ("little beams"). These are arranged along the line of greatest stress to help make bones light, but strong.

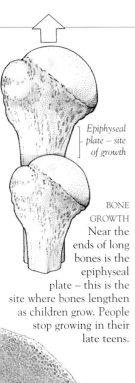

Epiphyseal plate – site of growth

BONE GROWTH
Near the ends of long bones is the epiphyseal plate – this is the site where bones lengthen as children grow. People stop growing in their late teens.

FRACTURES
A break in a bone forms a fracture. In an open (compound) fracture, the broken bone protrudes through the skin. In a closed (simple) fracture, the skin remains intact. Bone heals in several stages.

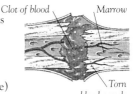

Clot of blood *Marrow* *Torn blood vessels*

1. A clot of blood fills the area of the fracture, 6–8 hours after the injury.

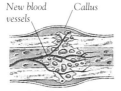

New blood vessels *Callus*

2. While blood capillaries grow into the blood clot, the damaged tissue is broken down and removed. Collagen fibres start to join up the broken ends of bone. Repair tissues form a swelling called a callus.

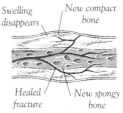

Swelling disappears *New compact bone* *Healed fracture* *New spongy bone*

3. Remodelling of the healing bone occurs. Repair tissue is replaced with spongy bone. Compact bone forms around the outer edge of the fracture.

BONE STRUCTURE
The skeleton has two types of bone. Compact bone, made up of tiny tubes of bone (osteons), forms the strong outer shell. Spongy bone makes up a lighter inner layer. Bone marrow is often found within spongy bone and the central space (medullary cavity) of long bones. Red marrow makes blood cells, while yellow marrow stores fat.

FACT BOX

• 99% of the body's calcium is in the bones and teeth.

• 75% of the body's bone is compact and 25% is spongy bone.

• Compact bone is the body's second hardest material after enamel.

21

THE SKULL

THE MOST COMPLICATED part of the skeleton is the
skull. It protects the most important sense organs,
and the cranial vault encases the brain. The bones of
the face provide anchorage for muscles involved in
facial expressions, talking, and chewing.

FRONT VIEW OF SKULL
All the bones of the skull,
except the lower jaw, are
locked together to make
a strong box, and
cannot move. The
special joints
between the skull
bones are called
sutures.

*Temporal
(temple) bone*

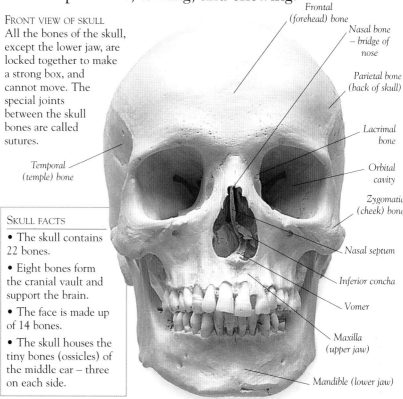

*Frontal
(forehead) bone*

*Nasal bone
– bridge of
nose*

*Parietal bone
(back of skull)*

*Lacrimal
bone*

*Orbital
cavity*

*Zygomatic
(cheek) bone*

Nasal septum

Inferior concha

Vomer

*Maxilla
(upper jaw)*

Mandible (lower jaw)

SKULL FACTS

• The skull contains
22 bones.

• Eight bones form
the cranial vault and
support the brain.

• The face is made up
of 14 bones.

• The skull houses the
tiny bones (ossicles) of
the middle ear – three
on each side.

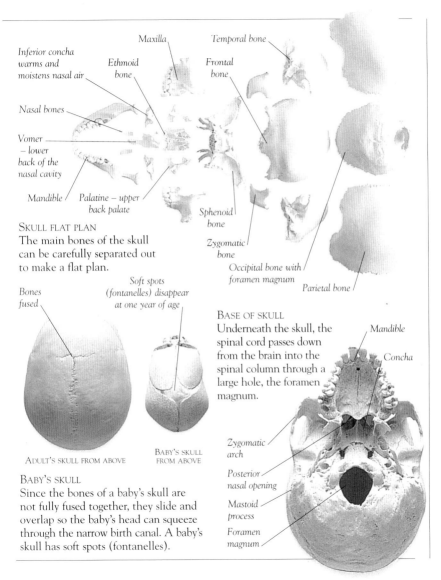

Maxilla

Temporal bone

Inferior concha
warms and
moistens nasal air

Ethmoid
bone

Frontal
bone

Nasal bones

Vomer
– lower
back of the
nasal cavity

Mandible / Palatine – upper
back palate

Sphenoid
bone

Zygomatic
bone

Occipital bone with
foramen magnum

Parietal bone

SKULL FLAT PLAN
The main bones of the skull
can be carefully separated out
to make a flat plan.

Soft spots
(fontanelles) disappear
at one year of age

Bones
fused

BASE OF SKULL
Underneath the skull, the
spinal cord passes down
from the brain into the
spinal column through a
large hole, the foramen
magnum.

Mandible

Concha

Zygomatic
arch

ADULT'S SKULL FROM ABOVE

BABY'S SKULL
FROM ABOVE

Posterior
nasal opening

BABY'S SKULL
Since the bones of a baby's skull are
not fully fused together, they slide and
overlap so the baby's head can squeeze
through the narrow birth canal. A baby's
skull has soft spots (fontanelles).

Mastoid
process

Foramen
magnum

23

THE SPINE

THE SPINAL COLUMN is one of the body's main supports. It is made up of 33 bones called vertebrae, which surround the spinal cord. The vertebrae interlock in a series of sliding joints that give the backbone flexibility. The spine has four gentle curves to give extra strength and stability.

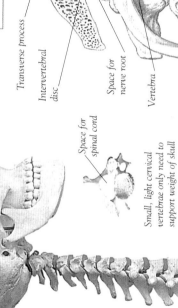

SKULL AND
SPINAL
COLUMN

The first cervical vertebra, the atlas, supports the skull, allowing it free movement

Spinous process

Dens

The second cervical vertebrae, the axis, has a peg that allows the atlas and skull to rotate and move up and down

Space for spinal cord

Small, light cervical vertebrae only need to support weight of skull

Transverse process

Intervertebral disc

Space for nerve root

Vertebra

SPINAL FACTS

- A human neck has the same number of vertebrae as a giraffe.
- Spinous processes form knobbles that protrude under the skin covering the spine.
- Intervertebral discs act as shock absorbers to prevent damage from sudden jolts.

Cancellous bone

Rib

INTERVERTEBRAL DISCS
The vertebrae are separated from each other by pads of cartilage, intervertebral discs. These have a tough, flexible outer case and a soft, jelly-like centre, and cushion and protect the vertebrae.

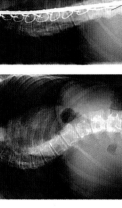

BEFORE   X-ray of excessive curvature of spine

AFTER   Inserting a stainless steel rod helps to straighten spine

CURVATURE OF THE SPINE
Spinal curves can become abnormally pronounced. Excessive curvature may be inwards in the lower back, outwards in the upper back, or to one side. An operation that inserts a rod may straighten the spine.

Centrum (body)

Each thoracic vertebra has two small hollows on either side to connect with a rib

Transverse process

Lumbar vertebrae are the strongest; they must support the weight of the upper body

Sacrum

Coccyx

VERTEBRA
The weight-bearing area of each vertebra is the centrum. This is attached to a ring of bone, the vertebral arch, which protects the spinal cord. Bony projections (processes) extend from the arch; the transverse processes form sliding joints.

JOINTS

TWO BONES MEET at a joint and are often held together by bands of tissue (ligaments). Some joints are fixed, with the bones locked together. In others, the bones can move more freely; cartilage protects their surfaces, which are lubricated by synovial fluid.

MOBILE JOINTS
The skeleton contains six main types of movable joint. "Double-jointed" people have a wider range of movement than usual due to looser ligaments.

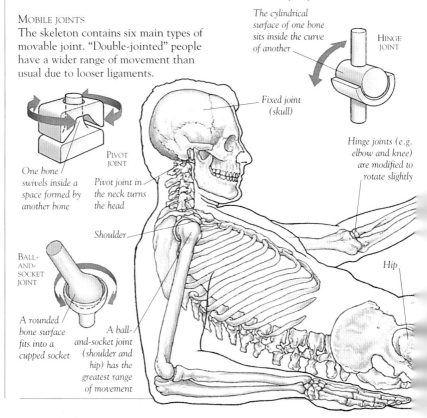

The cylindrical surface of one bone sits inside the curve of another

HINGE JOINT

Fixed joint (skull)

Hinge joints (e.g. elbow and knee) are modified to rotate slightly

PIVOT JOINT

One bone swivels inside a space formed by another bone

Pivot joint in the neck turns the head

Shoulder

Hip

BALL-AND-SOCKET JOINT

A rounded bone surface fits into a cupped socket

A ball-and-socket joint (shoulder and hip) has the greatest range of movement

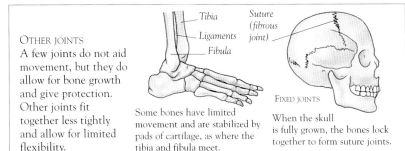

OTHER JOINTS
A few joints do not aid movement, but they do allow for bone growth and give protection. Other joints fit together less tightly and allow for limited flexibility.

Tibia
Ligaments
Fibula

Some bones have limited movement and are stabilized by pads of cartilage, as where the tibia and fibula meet.

Suture (fibrous joint)

FIXED JOINTS

When the skull is fully grown, the bones lock together to form suture joints.

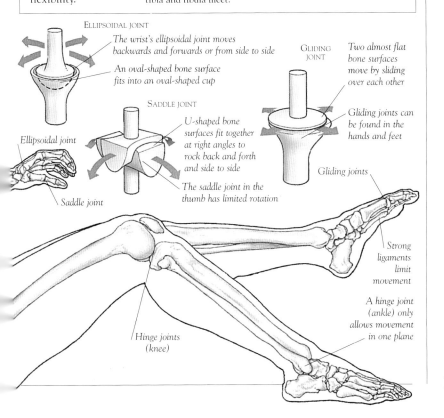

ELLIPSOIDAL JOINT
The wrist's ellipsoidal joint moves backwards and forwards or from side to side

An oval-shaped bone surface fits into an oval-shaped cup

Ellipsoidal joint

SADDLE JOINT
U-shaped bone surfaces fit together at right angles to rock back and forth and side to side

The saddle joint in the thumb has limited rotation

Saddle joint

GLIDING JOINT
Two almost flat bone surfaces move by sliding over each other

Gliding joints can be found in the hands and feet

Gliding joints

Strong ligaments limit movement

A hinge joint (ankle) only allows movement in one plane

Hinge joints (knee)

27

Joints and movement

Joints and muscles give the body a wide range of movement. Bending a joint, such as an elbow, is known as flexion. Straightening the joint again is known as extension. Moving part of the body, such as an arm, away from the body's midline is called abduction, while drawing the arm inwards is called adduction.

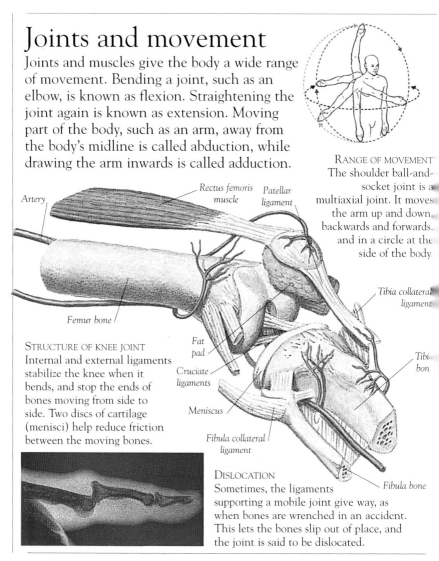

RANGE OF MOVEMENT
The shoulder ball-and-socket joint is a multiaxial joint. It moves the arm up and down, backwards and forwards, and in a circle at the side of the body

Artery

Rectus femoris muscle

Patellar ligament

Tibia collateral ligament

Femur bone

Tibia bone

STRUCTURE OF KNEE JOINT
Internal and external ligaments stabilize the knee when it bends, and stop the ends of bones moving from side to side. Two discs of cartilage (menisci) help reduce friction between the moving bones.

Fat pad

Cruciate ligaments

Meniscus

Fibula collateral ligament

DISLOCATION
Sometimes, the ligaments supporting a mobile joint give way, as when bones are wrenched in an accident. This lets the bones slip out of place, and the joint is said to be dislocated.

Fibula bone

ARTHRITIS

Inflammation of a joint leads to pain, swelling, and deformity and is called arthritis. Rheumatoid arthritis often affects small joints; the synovial membrane becomes inflamed and later thickens.

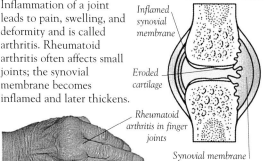

EARLY STAGE   LATE STAGE

Inflamed synovial membrane

Eroded cartilage

Rheumatoid arthritis in finger joints

Synovial membrane thickens and spreads across joint

JOINT FACTS

• The knee is the body's largest joint.

• The smallest joints link the three bones in the middle ear.

• Most large, movable joints are lubricated by synovial fluid.

• Muscles around the joints contract to produce movement.

STAGES IN OSTEOARTHRITIS

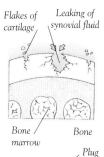

Flakes of cartilage   *Leaking of synovial fluid*

Bone marrow   *Bone*

STAGE 1

When the cartilage of a joint breaks down, it is known as osteoarthritis. It usually affects the larger, weight-bearing joints such as hips and knees.

Plug

Blood vessels

STAGE 2

Cracks in the cartilage develop and extend into the underlying bone. Blood vessels grow into the gap and secrete a clot that acts as a plug.

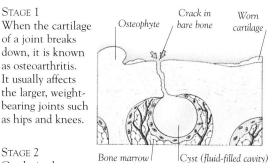

Osteophyte   *Crack in bare bone*   *Worn cartilage*

Bone marrow   *Cyst (fluid-filled cavity)*

STAGE 3

The plug wears away, allowing synovial fluid to leak in to form a cyst. The damaged bone forms swellings (osteophytes) and it becomes increasingly painful, stiff, and difficult to move the joint.

MUSCULAR SYSTEM

MUSCLES CARRY OUT all the body's voluntary and involuntary movements. Skeletal (voluntary) muscles are attached to bones either directly or through strong tendons. They tend to work in pairs; one muscle contracts while the other relaxes. This allows joints, such as the elbow, to bend or straighten.

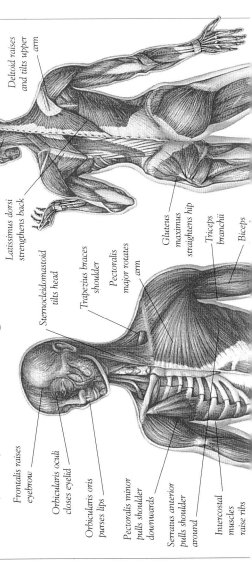

Semispinalis capitis tilts heads upwards

Deltoid raises and tilts upper arm

Trapezius pulls back head

Latissimus dorsi strengthens back

Gluteus maximus straightens hip

Triceps branchii

Biceps

Sternocleidomastoid tilts head

Trapezius braces shoulder

Pectoralis major rotates arm

Frontalis raises eyebrow

Orbicularis oculi closes eyelid

Orbicularis oris purses lips

Pectoralis minor pulls shoulder downwards

Serratus anterior pulls shoulder around

Intercostal muscles raise ribs

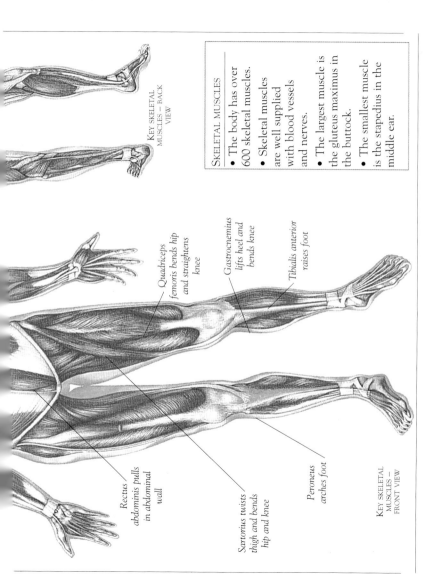

KEY SKELETAL MUSCLES – BACK VIEW

SKELETAL MUSCLES

- The body has over 600 skeletal muscles.

- Skeletal muscles are well supplied with blood vessels and nerves.

- The largest muscle is the gluteus maximus in the buttock.

- The smallest muscle is the stapedius in the middle ear.

Quadriceps femoris bends hip and straightens knee

Gastrocnemius lifts heel and bends knee

Tibialis anterior raises foot

Rectus abdominis pulls in abdominal wall

Sartorius twists thigh and bends hip and knee

Peroneus arches foot

KEY SKELETAL MUSCLES – FRONT VIEW

Muscle structures

About 40 per cent of body weight is made up of muscles. They carry out all the body's movements. Muscles have long, thin cells that convert chemical energy, found in fatty acids and blood sugar (glucose), into movement and heat. Some muscles are under voluntary control and only work consciously. Others function automatically to keep the body working smoothly.

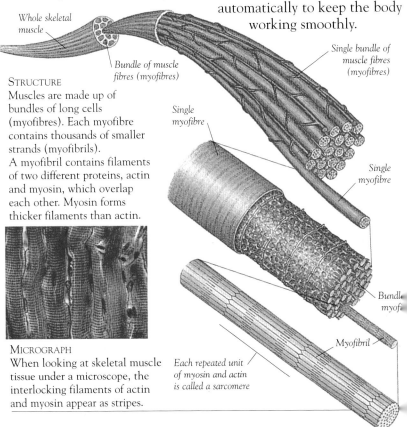

Whole skeletal muscle

Bundle of muscle fibres (myofibres)

Single bundle of muscle fibres (myofibres)

Single myofibre

Single myofibre

Bundle myofi...

Myofibril

Each repeated unit of myosin and actin is called a sarcomere

STRUCTURE

Muscles are made up of bundles of long cells (myofibres). Each myofibre contains thousands of smaller strands (myofibrils). A myofibril contains filaments of two different proteins, actin and myosin, which overlap each other. Myosin forms thicker filaments than actin.

MICROGRAPH

When looking at skeletal muscle tissue under a microscope, the interlocking filaments of actin and myosin appear as stripes.

TYPES OF MUSCLE

THREE TYPES OF MUSCLE

Skeletal muscle is known as voluntary muscle; its movements are controlled consciously. Cardiac muscle is found only in the heart. Smooth muscle is known as involuntary muscle and is responsible for automatic movements within the body.

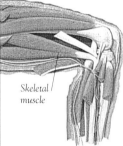

Skeletal muscle

SKELETAL MUSCLES

While some muscles attached to the skeleton contract, others relax to produce voluntary movements, such as walking and writing.

CARDIAC MUSCLES

Muscle in the heart has branched fibres. These help electrical signals to pass through quickly, causing the heart to contract rhythmically and tirelessly.

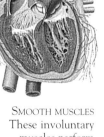

Cardiac muscle

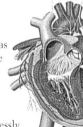

Smooth muscle in stomach

SMOOTH MUSCLES

These involuntary muscles perform automatic tasks, such as dilating or constricting blood vessels and propelling food through the stomach and gut.

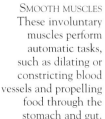

Tendon of semitendinosus muscle

Tendon of biceps femoris muscle

Skeletal muscle tapers into tendon

Achilles tendon

TENDONS

Skeletal muscle is attached to bones and other muscles through tendons. These are made of strong connective tissue.

MUSCLE FACTS

• Muscles can cause eyelids to blink up to five times per second.

• If too little oxygen reaches the muscles during strenuous exercise, waste lactic acid builds up, causing the muscles to ache.

Muscle action

Muscles can only pull, not push. Nerve signals from the brain instruct which muscle fibres to contract and when. For example, to pick up a weight, muscle fibres contract to produce a steady pull (isotonic contraction). To hold the weight steady once it has been picked up, muscle fibres stay the same length to produce tension (isometric contraction).

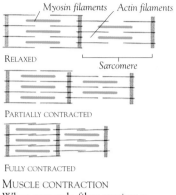

RELAXED

PARTIALLY CONTRACTED

FULLY CONTRACTED

MUSCLE CONTRACTION
When a muscle fibre receives a signal, its filaments slide over each other. The fibres shorten and the muscle contracts. As the filaments slide apart again, the muscle relaxes.

MUSCLES WORKING TOGETHER
As muscles can only pull, not push, they work in pairs to move joints. To raise the lower arm, the biceps muscle contracts while the triceps muscle relaxes.

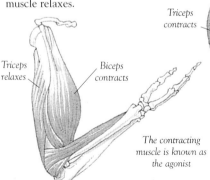

Triceps relaxes

Biceps contracts

The contracting muscle is known as the agonist

The relaxing muscle is known as the antagonist

Triceps contracts

To bring the lower arm down again, the triceps contracts and the biceps relaxes

Elbow joint straightens when biceps relaxes

BUILDING UP MUSCLE

Bodybuilders exercise their muscles repeatedly to build up their bulk. Each muscle becomes highly toned with strong tendons and an increased blood supply. Eating starchy foods and proteins helps increase bulk.

Highly developed muscles

FEMALE BODYBUILDER

TORN MUSCLE

Excessive strain on a muscle can damage muscle fibres. This causes pain, swelling, and loss of movement. When a muscle tears, the rich network of blood vessels in the muscle bleeds. If the blood builds up, it may need to be drained.

Deltoid muscle

Muscle tear due to excessive movements of shoulder joint

Humerus bone

FACIAL MUSCLES

FACIAL MUSCLES
The face has over 30 muscles, which relax and contract to express a variety of emotions from pleasure and surprise to anger and confusion.

FROWNING
Muscles (corrugator supercilii) above each eye pull the forehead down into a frown.

SURPRISE
A large muscle in the forehead (frontalis) contracts to raise the eyebrows in surprise.

GLUMNESS
A large, flat sheet of muscle (platysma) fans out down the neck and pulls the mouth down.

MUSCLE PROBLEMS	
PROBLEM	DESCRIPTION
Myalgia	Muscle pain due to infection or inflammation.
Tendinitis	Inflammation of a tendon due to over use or injury.
Cramp	Prolonged spasm due to the build-up of waste lactic acid.
Tetanus	Prolonged spasm due to a bacterial infection.
Muscular dystrophy	An inherited wasting disease.

HAIR AND NAILS

THE SKIN PRODUCES specialized structures made of the tough protein, keratin. Nails strengthen and shield the tips of fingers and toes. Hair provides warmth, and protects most areas of the skin.

STRUCTURE
The outer surface of each hair is coated with dead cells that protect the hair.

HAIR TYPES
Whether hair grows straight, wavy, or curly depends on the shape of the hair follicle.

Curly hair grows from an oval follicle

Wavy hair grows from a flat follicle

Straight hair grows from a round follicle

Hair sheath projects above skin's outer layer (epidermis)

Dermis

Erector muscle

Follicle (hair pit)

HAIR FOLLICLES
Hairs are tubes of keratin that grow from follicles in the lower layer (dermis) of the skin. There are about 100,000 hair follicles on the head.

BALDNESS
Male-pattern baldness can be inherited, but most men start to lose their hair as they get older. Hair often starts to recede from the front or the crown.

Receding hairline forms "widow's peak" at the front

Hair also starts to recede from the crown

Hair loss meets to produce baldness over the top of the head

NAIL STRUCTURE

Keratin, the hard, fibrous protein that makes up nails, is produced by active cells at the base and sides of each nail. These growing areas are protected by folds of skin, called cuticles.

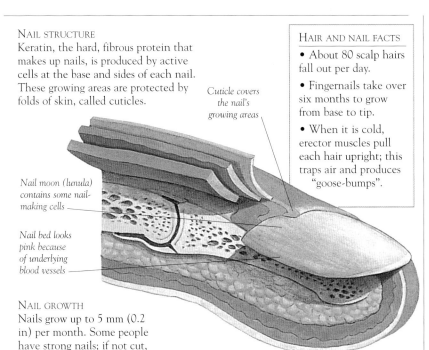

Cuticle covers the nail's growing areas

Nail moon (lunula) contains some nail-making cells

Nail bed looks pink because of underlying blood vessels

NAIL GROWTH

Nails grow up to 5 mm (0.2 in) per month. Some people have strong nails; if not cut, they can grow up to 30 cm (12 in) long.

SOME NAIL AND HAIR PROBLEMS	
NAME	DESCRIPTION
Whitlows	Small abscesses at the side of the nail.
Black nails	Hard knocks cause bruising and black nails.
Fungal infection	Fungus grows through the nail plate, making it brittle and distorted.
Brittle nails	Nails split and break easily, sometimes due to lack of iron.
Alopecia universalis	Loss of hair extends all over the body, including eyebrows and eyelashes.
Alopecia areata	Loss of hair produces one or more patches of baldness on the scalp. May be caused by emotional stress.

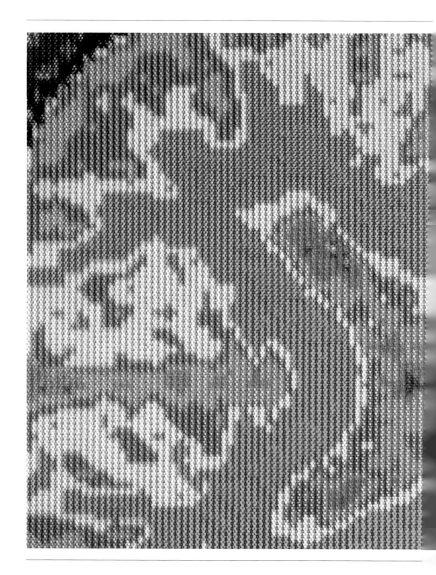

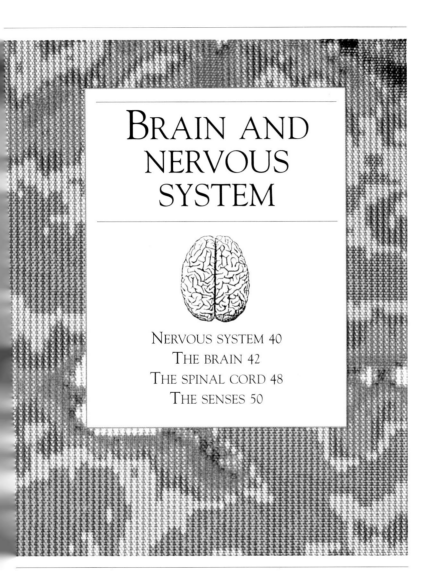

BRAIN AND NERVOUS SYSTEM

NERVOUS SYSTEM

THE BRAIN and the spinal cord make up the central nervous system (CNS). This interlinks with the peripheral nervous system, which forms a network of nerve fibres throughout the rest of the body.

These two systems work together to co-ordinate the body's actions.

NERVE FACTS

- All the body's nerves laid end to end would measure about 75 km (47 miles).
- The sciatic nerve is the longest nerve.
- Nerve signals can travel at over 400 km/h (248 mph).
- Pain signals travel more slowly than touch signals.

NERVE NETWORK
Nerve fibres run together in cables to form nerve trunks. These divide and branch into smaller nerves reaching every part of the body. Some nerves group together and interweave to form a plexus.

Optic nerve

Branchial plexus

Radial nerve

Vagus nerve

Phrenic nerve

Lateral pectoral nerve

Intercostal nerves

Subcostal nerve

Iliohypogastric nerve

Supraclavicular nerve

Axillary nerve

Radial nerve

Spinal ganglion

Spinal cord

Filum terminale

Femoral nerve

Gluteal nerve

Ulnar nerve

Common palmar digital nerve

Pudendal nerve

Sciatic nerve

Common peroneal nerve

Interosseous nerve

Deep peroneal nerve

Dorsal cutaneous nerves

Saphenous nerve

Tibial nerve

Superficial peroneal nerve

Lateral plantar nerve

PERIPHERAL NERVOUS SYSTEM

The peripheral nervous system has three main divisions: autonomic, sensory, and motor.

MAIN DIVISIONS	ACTION
Autonomic nerves	• Autonomic nerves control the body's involuntary movements. • They carry information from the central nervous system to the organs, glands, and blood. • There are two types of autonomic nerve: sympathetic and parasympathetic. They have opposing actions.
Sensory nerves	• Sensory nerves pass information from the sense receptors in the body back to the CNS.
Motor nerves	• Motor nerves control the body's voluntary movements. • They send signals from the CNS to the skeletal muscles, instructing them when to relax or contract.

41

THE BRAIN

THE BODY'S MAIN control centre is the brain. It is encased in the bony skull and floats in a pool of cerebrospinal fluid, which gives extra protection by absorbing shock waves. The brain communicates with the rest of the body through the cranial nerves and the spinal cord.

LEFT   RIGHT

HEMISPHERES
The brain is made up of two halves: the right and left hemispheres. The left side is usually dominant and controls logic and speech, while the right side producescreative thoughts.

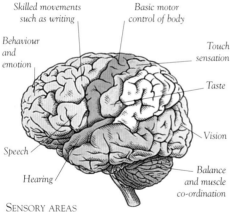

Skilled movements such as writing

Basic motor control of body

Behaviour and emotion

Touch sensation

Taste

Vision

Speech

Balance and muscle co-ordination

Hearing

Right cerebral hemisphere

White matter – made up of nerve fibres

Protective skull

Nasal cavity

Grey matter (cortex) – made up of nerve cell bodies

SENSORY AREAS
The brain is divided into several regions – each has its own important function. Some regions, known as sensory areas, receive information from sense organs and receptors. They are involved in interpreting sensations. Other parts, known as motor areas, control the movement of voluntary muscles.

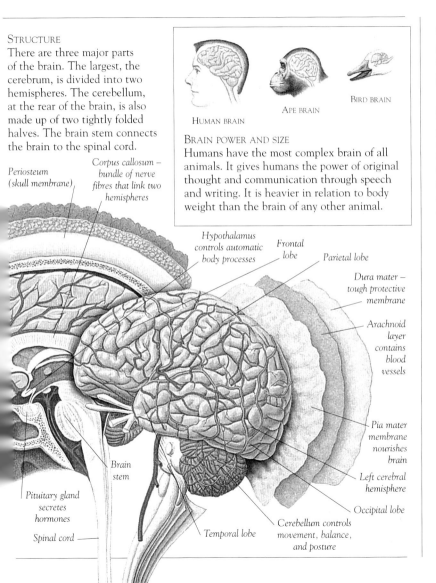

STRUCTURE

There are three major parts of the brain. The largest, the cerebrum, is divided into two hemispheres. The cerebellum, at the rear of the brain, is also made up of two tightly folded halves. The brain stem connects the brain to the spinal cord.

HUMAN BRAIN

APE BRAIN

BIRD BRAIN

BRAIN POWER AND SIZE

Humans have the most complex brain of all animals. It gives humans the power of original thought and communication through speech and writing. It is heavier in relation to body weight than the brain of any other animal.

Periosteum (skull membrane)

Corpus callosum – bundle of nerve fibres that link two hemispheres

Hypothalamus controls automatic body processes

Frontal lobe

Parietal lobe

Dura mater – tough protective membrane

Arachnoid layer contains blood vessels

Pia mater membrane nourishes brain

Left cerebral hemisphere

Occipital lobe

Brain stem

Pituitary gland secretes hormones

Spinal cord

Temporal lobe

Cerebellum controls movement, balance, and posture

43

Neurons

The nervous system has specialized cells called neurons, which carry electrical (nerve) impulses. Motor neurons transport signals from the brain and spinal cord, and sensory neurons carry signals from the body to the central nervous system.

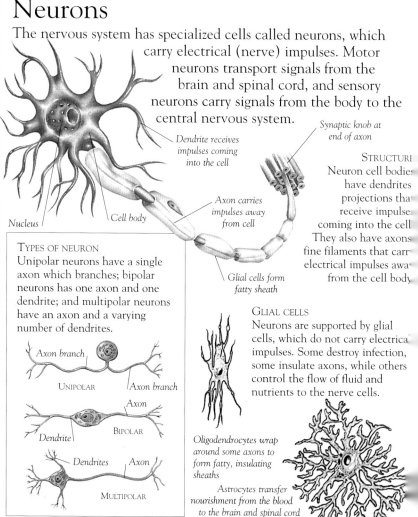

Synaptic knob at end of axon

Dendrite receives impulses coming into the cell

Axon carries impulses away from cell

Nucleus

Cell body

Glial cells form fatty sheath

STRUCTURE
Neuron cell bodies have dendrites projections that receive impulses coming into the cell. They also have axons, fine filaments that carry electrical impulses away from the cell body.

TYPES OF NEURON
Unipolar neurons have a single axon which branches; bipolar neurons has one axon and one dendrite; and multipolar neurons have an axon and a varying number of dendrites.

Axon branch

UNIPOLAR

Axon branch

Axon

Dendrite

BIPOLAR

Dendrites

Axon

MULTIPOLAR

GLIAL CELLS
Neurons are supported by glial cells, which do not carry electrical impulses. Some destroy infection, some insulate axons, while others control the flow of fluid and nutrients to the nerve cells.

Oligodendrocytes wrap around some axons to form fatty, insulating sheaths

Astrocytes transfer nourishment from the blood to the brain and spinal cord

44

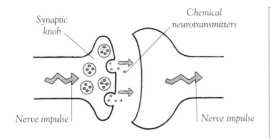

Synaptic knob

Chemical neurotransmitters

Nerve impulse

Nerve impulse

SYNAPSE
An axon of one cell meets a dendrite of another at a tiny gap called a synapse. Here nerve impulses are converted into chemical neurotransmitters. Once across the synapse, they change back into electrical impulses.

BRAIN BEHAVIOUR
• One brain cell can connect to 25,000 other brain cells.

• Neurons cannot divide and multiply like other cells.

• When neurons die, they are not replaced.

• If a brain cell is deprived of oxygen, it dies after 5 minutes.

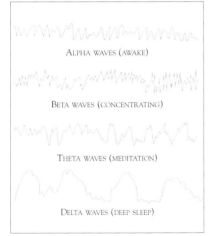

ALPHA WAVES (AWAKE)

BETA WAVES (CONCENTRATING)

THETA WAVES (MEDITATION)

DELTA WAVES (DEEP SLEEP)

BRAINWAVE RECORDINGS
Every second, millions of nerve impulses pass from neuron to neuron in the brain. This produces an electrical field; the brain's level of activity can be recorded as an electroencephalogram (EEG).

A baby needs 14–16 hours sleep a day

A three-year-old needs 12 hours sleep

An adult gets on average about 7.5 hours sleep each night

SLEEP
Neuron activity increases while the body sleeps. There are two types of sleep: rapid-eye-movement (REM) sleep, in which the eyes move constantly, and slow-wave sleep. There are four stages in slow-wave sleep – stage 1 is the lightest and stage 4 the deepest. Most dreaming occurs during REM sleep.

Cranial nerves

Twelve pairs of major nerves originate in the brain and its stem. These cranial nerves carry motor signals to muscles in the head and neck region, or carry sensory information back to the brain from the sense organs. Others control facial expressions.

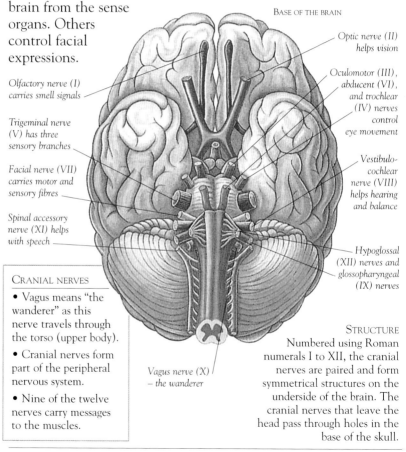

BASE OF THE BRAIN

Optic nerve (II) helps vision

Oculomotor (III), abducent (VI), and trochlear (IV) nerves control eye movement

Vestibulo-cochlear nerve (VIII) helps hearing and balance

Hypoglossal (XII) nerves and glossopharyngeal (IX) nerves

Olfactory nerve (I) carries smell signals

Trigeminal nerve (V) has three sensory branches

Facial nerve (VII) carries motor and sensory fibres

Spinal accessory nerve (XI) helps with speech

Vagus nerve (X) – the wanderer

CRANIAL NERVES

• Vagus means "the wanderer" as this nerve travels through the torso (upper body).

• Cranial nerves form part of the peripheral nervous system.

• Nine of the twelve nerves carry messages to the muscles.

STRUCTURE

Numbered using Roman numerals I to XII, the cranial nerves are paired and form symmetrical structures on the underside of the brain. The cranial nerves that leave the head pass through holes in the base of the skull.

CRANIAL NERVES

FUNCTIONS
Each nerve has a number
of important functions.
Some are involved in sight,
hearing, balance, smell, or
taste sensations.

BASE OF
THE BRAIN

Nerve carries information
from taste buds to the brain

Controls salivation,
tear production, and
facial muslces

FACIAL NERVE (VII)

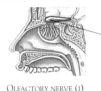
OLFACTORY NERVE (I)

Olfactory centre

Nerve carries
information from
smell receptors in the
nose to the olfactory
centre of the brain

Inner ear contains
sense organs

Nerves carry information
about hearing and balance
from the inner ear

VESTIBULOCOCHLEAR
NERVE (VIII)

OPTIC
NERVE
(II)

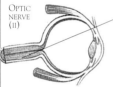

Nerve carries
information from
light receptors in
the retina of the
eye to visual
centres in the brain

Nerves control muscles
used in swallowing

Involved in taste, touch,
and temperature sensation
in the mouth

GLOSSOPHARYNGEAL (IX) AND
HYPOGLOSSAL NERVES (XII)

OCULOMOTOR (III),
TROCHLEAR (IV), AND
ABDUCENT NERVES
(VI)

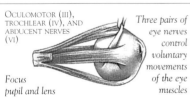

Focus
pupil and lens

Three pairs of
eye nerves
control
voluntary
movements
of the eye
muscles

Nerve regulates many
automatic functions such as
the heart rate, breathing, and
the making of stomach acid

Also involved in speech

VAGUS NERVE (X)

Each nerve has three
branches, which supply
sensation to parts of
the face and control
chewing muscles

TRIGEMINAL NERVE (V)

Nerve controls voluntary
muscles that move the
head and the neck

This nerve is also
involved in speech

SPINAL ACCESSORY NERVE (XI)

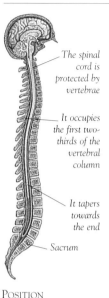

The spinal cord is protected by vertebrae

It occupies the first two-thirds of the vertebral column

It tapers towards the end

Sacrum

THE SPINAL CORD

A THICK BUNDLE of nerve fibres emerges through a hole (foramen magnum) in the base of the skull to form the spinal cord. Protected by cerebrospinal fluid, three membranes, and the bony vertebrae, the spinal cord extends from the brain. It relays information between the brain and various parts of the body.

POSITION
The spinal cord grows more slowly than the vertebral column, and only reaches about two-thirds of the way down the back in adults.

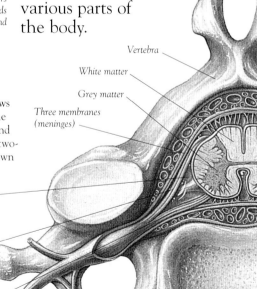

Vertebra

White matter

Grey matter

Three membranes (meninges)

Cerebrospinal fluid nourishes and cushions the spinal cord

Sensory nerve root leaves rear of cord

Motor nerve root leaves front of cord

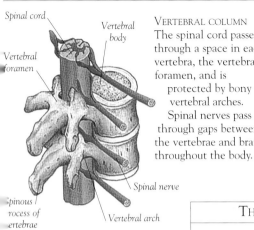

Spinal cord

Vertebral body

Vertebral foramen

Spinal nerve

Spinous process of vertebrae

Vertebral arch

VERTEBRAL COLUMN
The spinal cord passes through a space in each vertebra, the vertebral foramen, and is protected by bony vertebral arches. Spinal nerves pass through gaps between the vertebrae and branch throughout the body.

CROSS-SECTION
Grey matter, containing nerve cell bodies, and white matter, containing nerve cell filaments (axons) surrounded by fatty sheaths, make up the spinal cord. Sensory fibres from the rear of the cord join motor fibres from the front to form 31 pairs of spinal nerves.

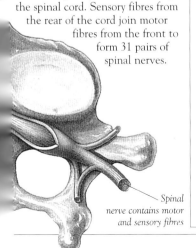

Spinal nerve contains motor and sensory fibres

THE KNEE-JERK REFLEX

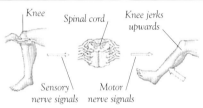

Knee

Spinal cord

Knee jerks upwards

Sensory nerve signals

Motor nerve signals

Stage 1
Tapping the tendon below the kneecap stretches the knee down.

Stage 2
Sensory stretch signals pass to spinal cord, and trigger reflex motor signals.

Stage 3
Muscles in the lower thigh contract, jerking the knee upwards.

REFLEX ARC
A spinal reflex is an involuntary response to a stimulus involving a nerve loop (reflex arc) that passes through the spinal cord. This produces a fast response to overcome possible dangers. Signals reach the brain several milliseconds later. A good example of a spinal reflex arc is the knee-jerk reflex of the lower leg.

THE SENSES

SENSORY RECEPTORS help to detect stimuli from inside and outside the body. As well as the five special senses of taste, smell, hearing, balance, and sight, there are other general senses, such as touch and pain.

The skin

Forming a waterproof barrier, the skin protects the body from physical damage and infection. It is also sensitive to touch, helps to control body temperature, and repairs itself.

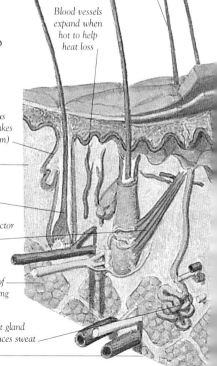

Movement of hair gives sensation of touch

Blood vessels expand when hot to help heat loss

Sebaceous gland makes oil (sebum)

Dermis

Hair follicle

Hair erector muscle

Layer of insulating fat

Sweat gland produces sweat

MERKEL'S DISC

FREE NERVE ENDING

RUFFINI'S CORPUSCLE

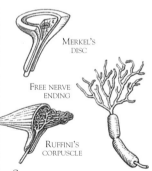

SENSORY NERVE ENDINGS
The skin contains a variety of nerve endings that detect light touch, sustained pressure, cold, warmth, or pain. They send electrical signals to the brain.

FINGERPRINTS

Months before birth, ridges of skin form on the fingertips. Arranged in unique patterns of whorls and loops, these ridges help to grip slippery surfaces and contain sweat ducts. No two people have the same fingerprints.

WHORL   ARCH

COMPOSITE   LOOP

SKIN FACTS

• The skin is the body's largest organ.

• The skin has a surface area of up to 2 m^2 (22 ft^2).

• The body sheds 18 kg (40 lb) of skin in an average lifetime.

• Household dust is mainly dead skin cells.

Epidermis contains layers of flattened skin cells

Basal layer of epidermis produces new cells

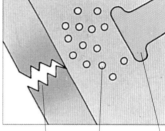

Damaged tissue | Chemicals | Nerve ending

PAIN RECEPTORS

When tissue is damaged, cells release chemicals. These activate the bare nerve endings that detect pain.

STRUCTURE

The skin has two main layers: an outer epidermis and an inner dermis. New cells move from the base of the epidermis to the surface, where they harden and die to produce a tough, waterproof layer. The dermis is living and contains nerves, blood vessels, sense receptors, glands, and hair follicles.

Sense receptor

51

The tongue

Used in talking, eating, and tasting, the tongue is a muscular structure. It contains taste buds that detect chemicals in food and drink. The tongue's sense of taste works with the nose's sense of smell to identify food flavours.

TONGUE SURFACE MAGNIFIED

STRUCTURE
Taste buds (receptor cells) are located on small bumps on the surface of the tongue, called papillae. They detect the four basic flavours – sweet, sour, bitter, and salty.

Bitterness is tasted at the back of the tongue

No taste buds in the centre

Sourness is tasted along the edges at the back

Saltiness is tasted along the sides at the front

Sweetness is tasted at the front

Taste pore   Taste hairs

TASTE FACTS

• A baby has taste buds all over the inside of the mouth.

• There are over 10,000 taste buds on the tongue.

• Taste bud cells only last a week before being renewed.

TASTE BUD
Sensory hairs project from cells into the central pore of the taste bud. Here, they dip into chemicals dissolved in saliva and detect any taste.

Nerve fibres

Tongue tissue

The nose

The sense of smell detects substances that release airborne molecules. These dissolve in nasal mucus and stimulate hair-like endings (cilia) inside the nose. Processed by the same part of the brain that deals with memory and emotions, smells can produce strong emotional responses.

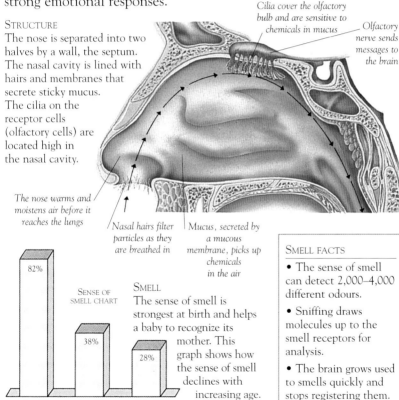

Cilia cover the olfactory bulb and are sensitive to chemicals in mucus

Olfactory nerve sends messages to the brain

STRUCTURE
The nose is separated into two halves by a wall, the septum. The nasal cavity is lined with hairs and membranes that secrete sticky mucus. The cilia on the receptor cells (olfactory cells) are located high in the nasal cavity.

The nose warms and moistens air before it reaches the lungs

Nasal hairs filter particles as they are breathed in

Mucus, secreted by a mucous membrane, picks up chemicals in the air

SENSE OF SMELL CHART

82% — AGE 20
38% — AGE 60
28% — AGE 80

SMELL
The sense of smell is strongest at birth and helps a baby to recognize its mother. This graph shows how the sense of smell declines with increasing age.

SMELL FACTS

• The sense of smell can detect 2,000–4,000 different odours.

• Sniffing draws molecules up to the smell receptors for analysis.

• The brain grows used to smells quickly and stops registering them.

The ear

The senses of hearing and balance involve the stimulation of hair receptor cells in the inner ear. Sounds are created by waves of pressure that cause air to vibrate. These vibrations trigger a chain of movement from the outer ear to the inner ear, where hair cells send electrical impulses to the brain for analysis.

EAR STRUCTURE

The ear is divided into three parts: the outer, middle, and inner ears. The outer ear consists of the pinna and auditory canal. The delicate parts of the ear are protected by the bones of the skull.

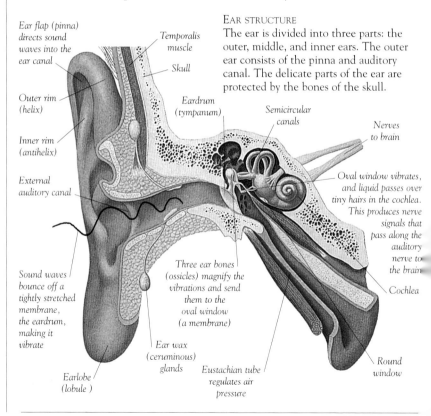

Ear flap (pinna) directs sound waves into the ear canal

Temporalis muscle

Skull

Outer rim (helix)

Eardrum (tympanum)

Semicircular canals

Nerves to brain

Inner rim (antihelix)

External auditory canal

Oval window vibrates, and liquid passes over tiny hairs in the cochlea. This produces nerve signals that pass along the auditory nerve to the brain

Cochlea

Sound waves bounce off a tightly stretched membrane, the eardrum, making it vibrate

Three ear bones (ossicles) magnify the vibrations and send them to the oval window (a membrane)

Ear wax (ceruminous) glands

Eustachian tube regulates air pressure

Round window

Earlobe (lobule)

MIDDLE EAR

Within this air-filled space are three tiny bones: the hammer (malleus), anvil (incus), and stirrup (stapes). Air pressure across the eardrum is regulated by the Eustachian tube, which links the middle ear to the throat.

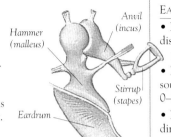

Hammer (malleus)

Anvil (incus)

Stirrup (stapes)

Eardrum

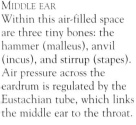

Fluid (perilymph) in labyrinth of channels

Nerves

Cochlea

Semicircular canals

EAR FACTS

- Humans can distinguish over 1,500 musical tones.

- People can hear sounds ranging from 0–140 decibels.

- Ears can detect the direction of sound within 3 degrees.

- The smallest bone in the body is the stirrup.

INNER EAR

The labyrinth, or inner ear, contains the sound-detecting cochlea and three semicircular canals. Hair cells sense motion and vibration, and send nerve impulses to the brain.

NOISE LEVELS

Loudness of sound is measured in decibels (dB). Sounds above 130dB can cause vibration damage to the ear and may lead to deafness.

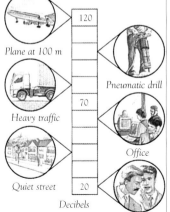

Plane at 100 m — 120

Pneumatic drill

Heavy traffic — 70

Office

Quiet street — 20

Whispering

Decibels

NOISE LEVEL COMPARISONS

BALANCE

Hair receptors respond to the flow of fluid within the semicircular canals. They detect changes in movement.

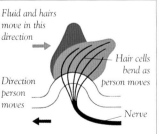

Fluid and hairs move in this direction

Hair cells bend as person moves

Direction person moves

Nerve

55

The eye

Sight is one of the most important senses. When light enters the eye, the lens focuses it upside-down onto the retina. The image stimulates light-sensitive cells called rods and cones, which send signals to the brain. Rods detect dim light but only register black and white. Cones give colour vision.

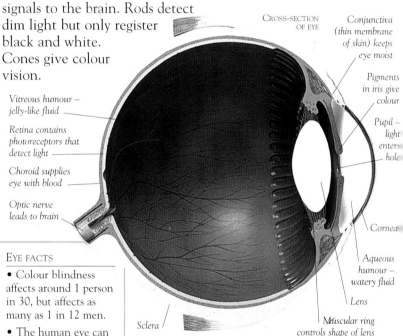

CROSS-SECTION OF EYE

Conjunctiva (thin membrane of skin) keeps eye moist

Pigments in iris give colour

Pupil – light enters hole

Vitreous humour – jelly-like fluid

Retina contains photoreceptors that detect light

Choroid supplies eye with blood

Optic nerve leads to brain

Cornea

Aqueous humour – watery fluid

Lens

Sclera

Muscular ring controls shape of lens

EYE FACTS

• Colour blindness affects around 1 person in 30, but affects as many as 1 in 12 men.

• The human eye can detect a lighted candle 1.6 km (1 mile) away.

• Humans blink about 15 times per minute.

• A person can see up to 10,000 colours.

EYE STRUCTURE
The spherical eyeball is divided by the lens into two fluid-filled compartments. Its surface has three layers: the tough outer sclera (white of eye); the choroid, composed of blood vessels; and the retina, containing light-sensitive cells. The transparent cornea protects the front of the eye and helps to focus light.

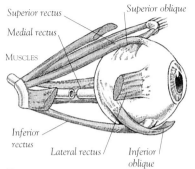

Superior rectus
Superior oblique
Medial rectus
MUSCLES
Inferior rectus
Lateral rectus
Inferior oblique

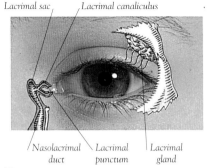

Lacrimal sac
Lacrimal canaliculus
Nasolacrimal duct
Lacrimal punctum
Lacrimal gland

EYE MOVEMENT

Six muscles attached to the sclera move the eyeball. Movements are co-ordinated so both eyes look in the same direction. If a muscle is weak, the eyes may move separately, causing a squint.

TEARS

The washing action of tears keeps the eyes moist and free from infection. Tears contain lysozyme, a chemical that helps to kill bacteria. Excess tears drain down the nasolacrimal duct into the nose.

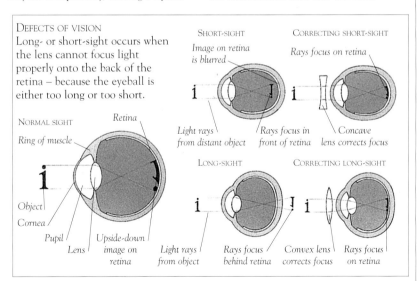

DEFECTS OF VISION

Long- or short-sight occurs when the lens cannot focus light properly onto the back of the retina – because the eyeball is either too long or too short.

NORMAL SIGHT
Retina
Ring of muscle
Object
Cornea
Pupil
Lens
Upside-down image on retina

SHORT-SIGHT
Image on retina is blurred
Light rays from distant object
Rays focus in front of retina

CORRECTING SHORT-SIGHT
Rays focus on retina
Concave lens corrects focus

LONG-SIGHT
Light rays from object
Rays focus behind retina

CORRECTING LONG-SIGHT
Convex lens corrects focus
Rays focus on retina

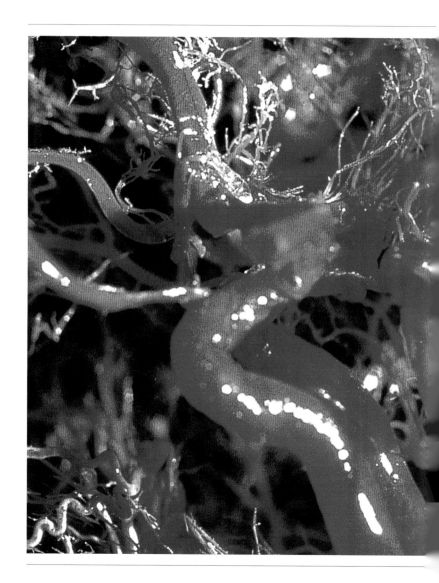

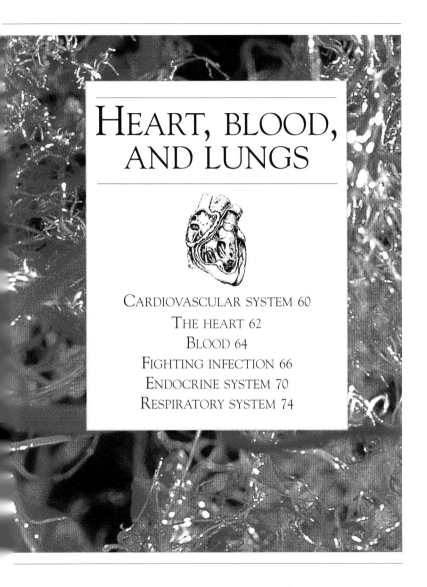

HEART, BLOOD, AND LUNGS

CARDIOVASCULAR SYSTEM

MADE UP OF THE HEART, blood, and blood vessels, the cardiovascular system supplies every part of the body with oxygen, nutrients, and chemicals that regulate the body's processes. It also carries away wastes and carbon dioxide. Arteries transport blood away from the heart, while veins carry blood to the heart.

BLOOD AND VESSELS
- The circulatory system contains around 150,000 km (93,000 miles) of blood vessels.
- The heart pumps about 13,640 litres (3,600 gallons) of blood per day.
- The aorta is the largest artery; the vena cava is the largest vein.

Temporal artery

Facial artery

Common carotid artery

External jugular vein

Thyroid vein

Axillary vein

Superior vena cava

Pulmonary arteries

Aorta

Heart

Descending aorta

Inferior vena cava

Superior

Radial artery

Ulnar artery

Pulmonary veins

Common hepatic artery

Gastric artery

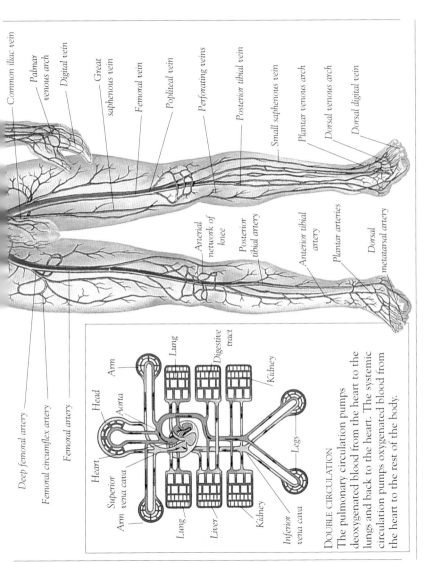

Common iliac vein
Palmar venous arch
Digital vein
Great saphenous vein
Femoral vein
Popliteal vein
Perforating veins
Posterior tibial vein
Small saphenous vein
Plantar venous arch
Dorsal venous arch
Dorsal digital vein

Deep femoral artery
Femoral circumflex artery
Femoral artery

Arterial network of knee
Posterior tibial artery
Anterior tibial artery
Plantar arteries
Dorsal metatarsal artery

Head
Arm
Aorta
Lung
Digestive tract
Kidney
Superior vena cava
Heart
Arm
Legs
Lung
Liver
Kidney
Inferior vena cava

DOUBLE CIRCULATION

The pulmonary circulation pumps deoxygenated blood from the heart to the lungs and back to the heart. The systemic circulation pumps oxygenated blood from the heart to the rest of the body.

THE HEART

ACTING AS A DOUBLE PUMP, the heart is a fist-sized muscular organ divided into a left and a right side. Each side contains two chambers: an upper atrium and a lower ventricle. These chambers contract and relax about 70 times a minute to keep blood flowing around the body.

THE HEART LIES IN THE MIDDLE OF THE CHEST

STRUCTURE

A thick, muscular wall called the septum separates the two sides of the heart. Although the atria have thinner walls than the ventricles, all the chambers hold the same volume of blood, 70–80 ml (2.5–2.8 fl oz).

OPEN VALVE   CLOSED VALVE

HEART VALVES

The four main heart valves (mitral, tricuspid, pulmonary, and aortic) open to let blood through, then close to prevent back-flow. This keeps blood moving in the same direction.

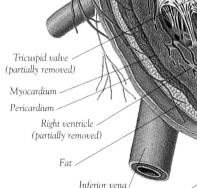

Superior vena cava

Right atrium

Pulmonary vein carries oxygenated blood

Tricuspid valve (partially removed)

Myocardium

Pericardium

Right ventricle (partially removed)

Fat

Inferior vena cava

Aorta

Artery to head

Cardiac nerves

Aorta

Pulmonary valve

Aortic valve

Pulmonary artery
carries deoxygenated
blood

HEARTBEAT CYCLE

Stage 1
During diastole (resting), both atria fill with blood. Some blood flows down into the ventricles below.

Stage 2
During atrial systole (pumping), both atria contract, forcing blood down into the ventricles.

Stage 3
During ventricular systole, both ventricles contract, pumping blood out into the body and lungs.

STAGE 1   STAGE 2   STAGE 3

ECG READING

HEART TRACE

An electrocardiograph records electrical activity in the heart using electrodes attached to the chest and limbs. This recording, which traces the heartbeat cycle, is called an electrocardiogram (ECG).

Mitral valve

Tendon
supporting valve

Coronary vein

Coronary artery

Septum

Left ventricle

Muscular column
supporting valve tendons

HEART FACTS

• The heart beats more than 30 million times a year.

• In an average lifetime of 70 years, the heart will be at rest for 40 years.

BLOOD

ALL TISSUES IN THE BODY receive a blood supply, even the bones. Blood is made up of plasma, a watery fluid in which float billions of red blood cells (erythrocytes), white blood cells (leucocytes), and cell fragments (platelets). Plasma also contains dissolved salts, hormones, fats, sugars, and proteins.

BLOOD CELLS
In order to supply the body with oxygen, red blood cells are shaped to squeeze through the narrowest blood vessel, a capillary.

Platelet

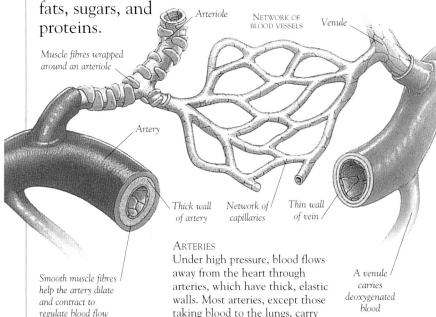

Muscle fibres wrapped around an arteriole

Arteriole

NETWORK OF BLOOD VESSELS

Venule

Artery

Thick wall of artery

Network of capillaries

Thin wall of vein

Smooth muscle fibres help the artery dilate and contract to regulate blood flow

ARTERIES
Under high pressure, blood flows away from the heart through arteries, which have thick, elastic walls. Most arteries, except those taking blood to the lungs, carry bright red, oxygenated blood.

A venule carries deoxygenated blood

VEINS

Carrying blood back to the heart under relatively low pressure, veins have thinner walls than arteries. Most veins, except those taking blood from the lungs, carry deoxygenated blood, which looks blue.

A venule is a small vein

Valve in the vein stops blood from flowing backwards

BLOOD FACTS

• There are four main blood groups: A, B, AB, and O.

• Oxygen binds with haemoglobin in red blood cells to give blood its red colour.

• The average body has about 5 litres (9 pints) of blood.

A venule branches off a vein

BLOOD VESSELS

Arteries branch into smaller arterioles connected to a web of capillaries. These have thin walls through which oxygen and nutrients can pass. The capillaries return deoxygenated blood to venules, which feed into larger vein trunks.

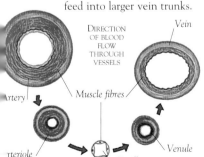

DIRECTION OF BLOOD FLOW THROUGH VESSELS

Vein

Artery

Muscle fibres

Arteriole

Capillary

Venule

BLOOD CLOTTING

When tissue is damaged, a clot forms to stop the bleeding.

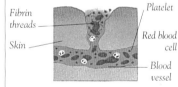

Fibrin threads

Skin

Platelet

Red blood cell

Blood vessel

Damaged tissues release chemicals that attract platelets. These stick together and trigger the formation of a fibrin web.

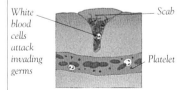

White blood cells attack invading germs

Scab

Platelet

Red blood cells become trapped in the web, forming a clot. This dries, leaving a scab to protect the healing wound.

CARDIOVASCULAR SYSTEM

FIGHTING INFECTION

THE BODY'S DEFENCES against infection include the skin barrier and the production of germ-fighting chemicals and cells. These immune cells patrol the whole body, but are concentrated in the lymphatic tissues. Fluid from blood drains into the body tissues and then into the lymphatic system, where it is filtered and returned to the bloodstream.

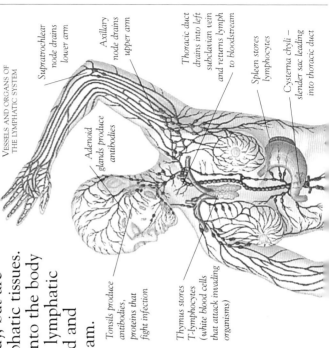

VESSELS AND ORGANS OF
THE LYMPHATIC SYSTEM

Supratrochlear node drains lower arm

Axillary node drains upper arm

Thoracic duct drains into left subclavian vein and returns lymph to bloodstream

Adenoid glands produce antibodies

Spleen stores lymphocytes

Cysterna chyli – slender sac leading into thoracic duct

Tonsils produce antibodies, proteins that fight infection

Thymus stores T-lymphocytes (white blood cells that attack invading organisms)

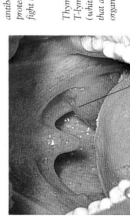

Tonsil

TONSILS
When infection is present in the mouth's lymphatic fluid, the tonsils swell and become painful as immune cells multiply to fight the invaders.

clusters of lymph
tissues known as
Peyer's patches

Bone marrow
produces
lymphocytes
(immune cells)

Popliteal lymph nodes
drain lower leg

Lymph capillaries
drain tissue fluids
into lymph system

IMMUNE FACTS

- Swollen glands are a sign of infection.
- Lymph nodes are most numerous in the armpits and groin.
- The spleen filters out infection and worn-out red blood cells.
- Chemicals in eye, stomach, and mouth fluids fight infection.

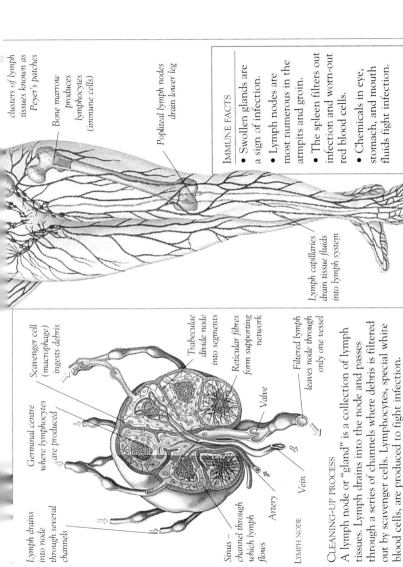

Lymph drains
into node
through several
channels

Germinal centre
where lymphocytes
are produced

Scavenger cell
(macrophage)
ingests debris

Trabeculae
divide node
into segments

Reticular fibres
form supporting
network

Valve

Filtered lymph
leaves node through
only one vessel

Sinus –
channel through
which lymph
flows

Artery

Vein

LYMPH NODE

CLEANING-UP PROCESS

A lymph node or "gland" is a collection of lymph tissues. Lymph drains into the node and passes through a series of channels where debris is filtered out by scavenger cells. Lymphocytes, special white blood cells, are produced to fight infection.

67

The immune system

Specialized immune cells are designed to protect against disease by attacking "foreign" invaders, including bacteria, viruses, and foreign proteins such as poisons and transplanted tissues. Body cells have distinctive membranes. This helps immune cells recognize and ignore normal cells, but destroy infected or cancerous ones.

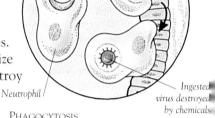

Neutrophil engulfs virus

Neutrophil

Ingested virus destroyed by chemicals

PHAGOCYTOSIS

Some immune cells, such as neutrophils and macrophages, can engulf invading organisms. This is known as phagocytosis.

WHITE BLOOD CELLS

All immune cells are made in the bone marrow or thymus gland. They secrete chemical alarm signals called cytokines. These quickly attract other patrolling immune cells into an area for a swift immune response.

NAME	FUNCTION
Neutrophils	Making up about 60% of circulating white blood cells, these engulf bacteria.
Macrophages	Scavenger cells hunt down and engulf unwanted tissue debris and foreign matter.
B-lymphocytes (B-cells)	Each B-lymphocyte makes a single, specific type of antibody.
T-lymphocytes (T-cells)	These control antibody production by B-cells and also attack infected cells.

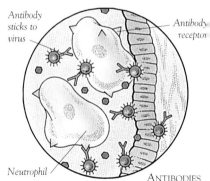

Antibody sticks to virus

Antibody receptor

Neutrophil

ANTIBODIES

B-cells make antibodies, which recognize and stick to invading organisms, such as a virus. These antibodies can stick to special receptors on neutrophils to speed up the process of phagocytosis.

IMMUNIZATION

Active immunization protects the body for years by injecting harmless extracts that mimic infection. Passive immunization injects antibodies taken from recently infected people and lasts only a few weeks.

ACTIVE IMMUNIZATION

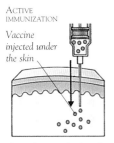

Vaccine injected under the skin

A vaccine contains harmless or dead organisms that cannot cause disease.

Antibody *Vaccine*

A vaccine stimulates the production of antibodies by B-cells.

Real infection

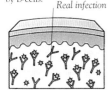

The vaccine allows for a more rapid immune response if the real disease is encountered.

PASSIVE IMMUNIZATION

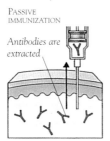

Antibodies are extracted

Volunteers donate blood containing antibodies.

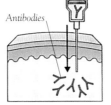

Antibodies

The donated antibodies are injected into the patient.

Real infection

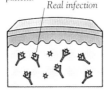

If disease organisms attack in the near future, the donated antibodies mop them up.

IMMUNE FACTS

- Neutrophils only live 6–20 hours.

- Macrophage literally means "big eater".

- B-lymphocytes are made in bone marrow.

- T-lymphocytes are derived from the thymus gland.

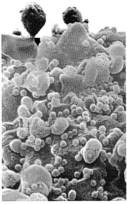

AIDS VIRUS

HIV (human immuno-deficiency virus) causes AIDS (acquired immune deficiency syndrome). T-helper cells, which help other immune cells to function, are attacked and their numbers fall. This weakens the body's fight against infection.

ENDOCRINE SYSTEM

THE BODY HAS TWO types of gland: exocrine glands, which secrete substances such as saliva through ducts, and ductless endocrine glands, which secrete hormones directly into the bloodstream. Hormones are chemical messengers that stimulate, regulate, and co-ordinate various processes and functions that occur within the body.

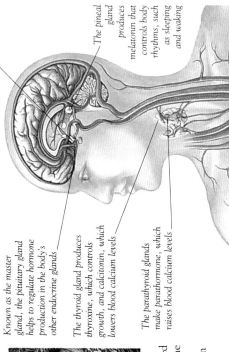

Hormones produced by the hypothalamus stimulate other glands to make and release their own hormones

The pineal gland produces melatonin that controls body rhythms, such as sleeping and waking

Known as the master gland, the pituitary gland helps to regulate hormone production in the body's other endocrine glands

The thyroid gland produces thyroxine, which controls growth, and calcitonin, which lowers blood calcium levels

The parathyroid glands make parathormone, which raises blood calcium levels

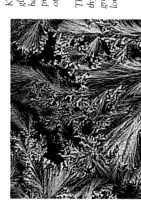

ADRENALINE CRYSTALS
Individual hormones can be crystallized and studied in a laboratory. Adrenaline hormone, secreted by the adrenal glands, works with the nervous system to prepare the body for fight or flight in stressful situations.

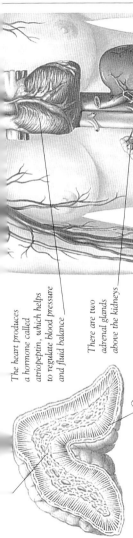

The heart produces a homone called atriopeptin, which helps to regulate blood pressure and fluid balance

There are two adrenal glands above the kidneys

The kidneys produce erythropoietin, which acts on bone marrow to increase the production of red blood cells

The pancreas produces glucagon and insulin that regulate blood sugar levels

The stomach and intestines secrete hormones that aid digestion

The ovary makes female sex hormones, progestogen and oestrogen, which prepare the female body for reproduction

Cortex

ADRENAL GLAND

The outer layer (cortex) of the adrenal gland produces hormones called corticosteroids, which help to control the metabolism (the body's chemical processes) and the concentration of salts in the blood. The inner medulla produces adrenaline.

ENDOCRINE FACTS

- Adrenaline gives superhuman strength in emergency situations.
- Too much growth hormone from the pituitary gland can produce gigantism (excessive growth).

The pituitary gland

Often referred to as the master gland, the pituitary is the most important endocrine gland. It produces its own hormones; these stimulate different endocrine glands to secrete other hormones. They also have a direct action on several body functions.

The pituitary gland hangs down from part of the brain called the hypothalamus, which links the nervous and endocrine systems.

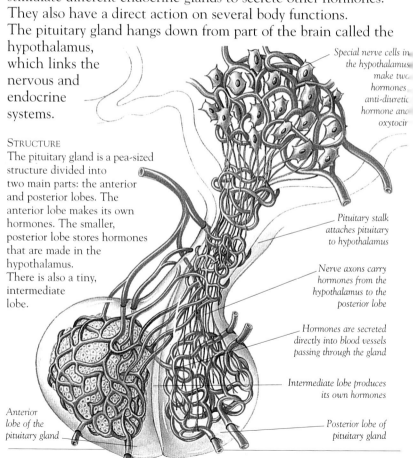

Special nerve cells in the hypothalamus make two hormones, anti-diuretic hormone and oxytocin

STRUCTURE

The pituitary gland is a pea-sized structure divided into two main parts: the anterior and posterior lobes. The anterior lobe makes its own hormones. The smaller, posterior lobe stores hormones that are made in the hypothalamus. There is also a tiny, intermediate lobe.

Pituitary stalk attaches pituitary to hypothalamus

Nerve axons carry hormones from the hypothalamus to the posterior lobe

Hormones are secreted directly into blood vessels passing through the gland

Intermediate lobe produces its own hormones

Anterior lobe of the pituitary gland

Posterior lobe of pituitary gland

EFFECTS OF SOME PITUITARY HORMONES

PITUITARY HORMONE	TARGET GLAND OR TISSUE	ACTION
ACTH Adrenocorticotropic hormone	ADRENAL GLAND	Stimulates the adrenal glands to produce steroid hormones. These regulate the metabolism of carbohydrates, fats, proteins, and minerals, and help the body adapt to stress.
Oxytocin and prolactin hormones	UTERINE MUSCLES AND MAMMARY GLANDS	These stimulate the breasts so that milk is produced after pregnancy for as long as the baby continues to feed. Oxytocin also stimulates the contraction of the uterus during childbirth.
TSH Thyroid-stimulating hormone	THYROID GLAND	Triggers production of hormones in the thyroid gland. These regulate the metabolic rate and growth. They also have an effect on the heart rate.
FSH AND LH Follicle-stimulating hormone and leuteinizing hormone	TESTIS AND OVARY	Both these pituitary hormones act on the sex glands (ovaries or testes) to stimulate the production of sex hormones. These glands control sexual development and the release of eggs or sperm.
ADH Anti-diuretic hormone (also known as vasopressin)	KIDNEY TUBULES	Has a direct action on the kidney to control the amount of water lost in the urine. ADH also causes small arteries to constrict when blood pressure is low.
MSH Melanocyte-stimulating hormone	SKIN	Has a direct action on pigment cells in the skin (melanocytes) to trigger the production of the tanning pigment, melanin, which provides some protection against the harmful effects of the sun's rays.
GH Growth hormone	BONE AND GENERAL GROWTH	Acts on the whole body to promote growth by stimulating the division of cells. It is vital for normal growth and development in children.

RESPIRATORY SYSTEM

A REGULAR SUPPLY of oxygen from the air is vital to life. Air enters the body through the nose and mouth, where it is filtered. It then passes down through the trachea (windpipe) into the lungs. The trachea has two main branches, the left and right bronchi, which divide into a network of smaller bronchioles. These lead into clusters of tiny air spaces, called alveoli.

THE LUNGS LIE IN THE MIDDLE OF THE CHEST

LARYNX
Made of cartilage, the larynx links the base of the throat to the trachea. A protective flap, the epiglottis, and the false vocal cords close the larynx to stop food going down the wrong way during swallowing.

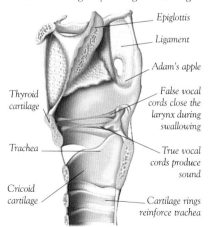

Epiglottis

Ligament

Adam's apple

Thyroid cartilage

False vocal cords close the larynx during swallowing

Trachea

True vocal cords produce sound

Cricoid cartilage

Cartilage rings reinforce trachea

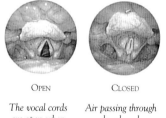

OPEN

CLOSED

The vocal cords are open when at rest

Air passing through closed cords produces sound

VOCAL CORDS
As air passes through the pair of fibrous vocal cords, they vibrate and make sounds. These are modulated by the mouth and tongue to produce speech. High-pitched sounds are made by tightening the cords. Deep sounds are made by loosening the vocal cords.

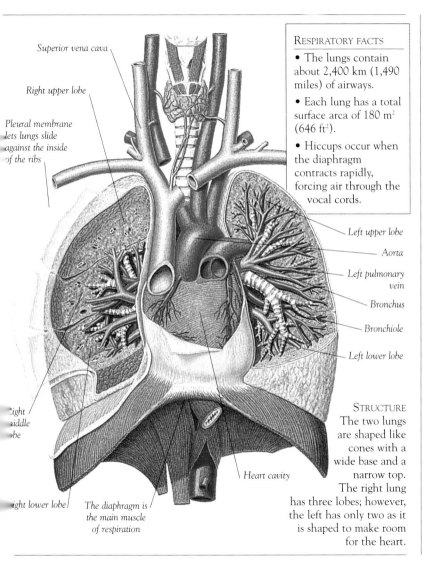

Superior vena cava

Right upper lobe

Pleural membrane
lets lungs slide
against the inside
of the ribs

Right
middle
lobe

Right lower lobe

The diaphragm is
the main muscle
of respiration

Heart cavity

Left upper lobe

Aorta

Left pulmonary
vein

Bronchus

Bronchiole

Left lower lobe

RESPIRATORY FACTS

- The lungs contain about 2,400 km (1,490 miles) of airways.
- Each lung has a total surface area of 180 m² (646 ft²).
- Hiccups occur when the diaphragm contracts rapidly, forcing air through the vocal cords.

STRUCTURE

The two lungs are shaped like cones with a wide base and a narrow top. The right lung has three lobes; however, the left has only two as it is shaped to make room for the heart.

Lung functions

Air is drawn in and out of the lungs by the contraction and relaxation of the diaphragm muscle. Once air reaches the lungs, oxygen is extracted and passes into the blood through the thin walls of microscopic air sacs (alveoli). It is exchanged for the body's waste product, carbon dioxide, which is exhaled (breathed out).

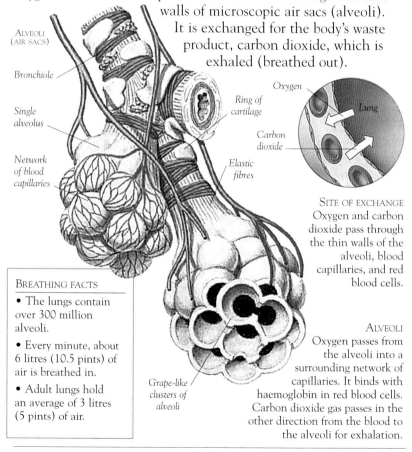

ALVEOLI
(AIR SACS)

Bronchiole

Single
alveolus

Network
of blood
capillaries

Ring of
cartilage

Elastic
fibres

Oxygen

Lung

Carbon
dioxide

Grape-like
clusters of
alveoli

SITE OF EXCHANGE
Oxygen and carbon dioxide pass through the thin walls of the alveoli, blood capillaries, and red blood cells.

ALVEOLI
Oxygen passes from the alveoli into a surrounding network of capillaries. It binds with haemoglobin in red blood cells. Carbon dioxide gas passes in the other direction from the blood to the alveoli for exhalation.

BREATHING FACTS

• The lungs contain over 300 million alveoli.

• Every minute, about 6 litres (10.5 pints) of air is breathed in.

• Adult lungs hold an average of 3 litres (5 pints) of air.

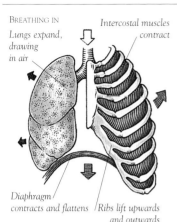

BREATHING IN

Lungs expand, drawing in air

Intercostal muscles contract

Diaphragm contracts and flattens

Ribs lift upwards and outwards

INHALATION

When the diaphragm contracts and the rib cage expands, pressure in the chest cavity lowers and air rushes into the lungs.

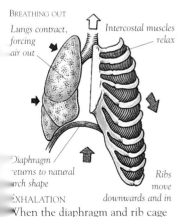

BREATHING OUT

Lungs contract, forcing air out

Intercostal muscles relax

Diaphragm returns to natural arch shape

Ribs move downwards and in

EXHALATION

When the diaphragm and rib cage relax, pressure in the chest increases, forcing air out again.

AIR COMPOSITION

Carbon dioxide 0.03%   Oxygen 21%

Nitrogen 78%

COMPOSITION OF INHALED AIR

Carbon dioxide 5%   Oxygen 16%

Nitrogen 79%

COMPOSITION OF EXHALED AIR

AIR Mouth-to-mouth resuscitation uses the oxygen in exhaled air to revive a person who has stopped breathing.

SMOKING

Cigarette smoke irritates the lungs and enters the bloodstream. Linked with 90 per cent of all cancers, smoking also increases the risk of high blood pressure, strokes, and other circulatory problems.

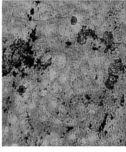

SMOKE DEPOSITS IN LUNG

COMMON RESPIRATORY PROBLEMS

NAME	DESCRIPTION
Asthma	Constricted bronchioles trigger coughing, wheezing, and breathlessness.
Acute bronchitis	Temporary inflammation of bronchi due to infection.
Chronic bronchitis	Long-term inflammation of airways due to smoking or pollution.
Emphysema	Breakdown of alveolar structure, often due to smoking, causes breathlessness.
Pneumonia	Alveoli fill with fluid and dead white blood cells due to bacterial infection.

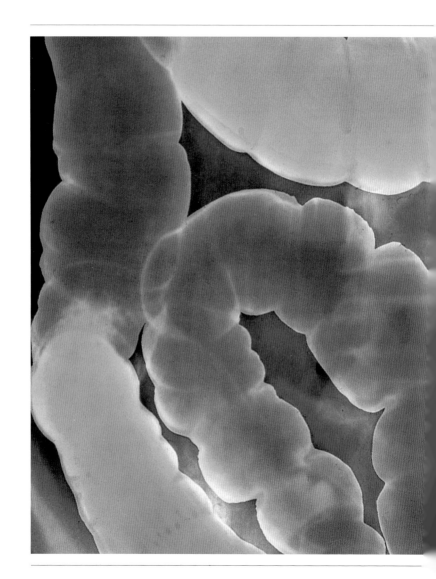

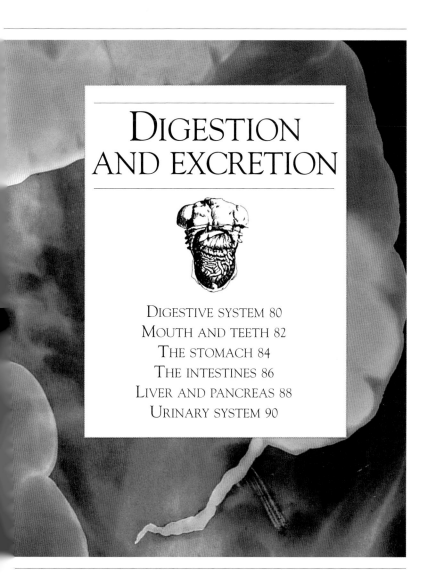

DIGESTION AND EXCRETION

DIGESTIVE SYSTEM

FOOD MUST be broken down into its basic components before the body can absorb and use its nutrients. This process of digestion starts with the mouth watering. As food passes through the body, it is broken down by enzymes – special proteins that accelerate the body's chemical reactions. Undigested waste is excreted as faeces.

Epiglottis stops fluid entering the trachea during swallowing

Food is broken down in the mouth by chewing

Salivary glands add enzymes that break down starch

Food is swallowed as a lump called a bolus

Waves of muscular action carry food down the oesophagus into the stomach

Food is churned, digested, and stored in the stomach

The liver makes bile that helps to break fat into tiny globules

The gallbladder stores bile until it is needed

The pancreas releases digestive enzymes that break down starch, fat, and protein

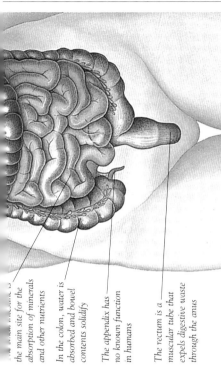

...the main site for the absorption of minerals and other nutrients

In the colon, water is absorbed and bowel contents solidify

The appendix has no known function in humans

The rectum is a muscular tube that expels digestive waste through the anus

The digestive tract runs from the mouth to the anus and is about 9 m (30 ft) long. Food passes from the mouth, down the oesophagus into the stomach. From here, it passes into the small intestine, made up of the duodenum, jejunum, and ileum, and into the large intestine, made up of the colon and rectum. Several organs and glands are connected to the tract to help digestion.

FOOD BREAK-DOWN

REGION/GLAND	SECRETION	ENZYME PRODUCED	FOOD ACTED ON	PRODUCT
Salivary glands (mouth)	Saliva	Amylase	Starch	Maltose
Gastric glands (stomach)	Gastric juices	Pepsin, lipase	Proteins, fats	Amino and fatty acids
Pancreas	Pancreatic juices	Trypsin, elastase, lipase, amylase	Proteins, fats, starch	Amino acids, fatty acids, maltose
Small intestine	Succus entericus	Sucrase, lactase, peptidase, lipase	Sucrose, lactose, proteins, fats	Galactose, amino and fatty acids
Colon (large intestine)	Bacterial secretions	Bacterial enzymes	Undigested vegetable fibre	Gases and fermentation products

DIGESTIVE SYSTEM

81

MOUTH AND TEETH

USED FOR MANY FUNCTIONS, including breathing and talking, the mouth is the entrance of the digestive tract. During eating, teeth cut and grind food to break it down. After saliva has lubricated the food, the tongue rolls it into a ball (bolus) and pushes it to the back of the mouth, ready for swallowing.

Pointed canine

Small premolar

Large molar

Sharp incisor

Gum acts as shock absorber

Tough enamel

Dentine – softer tissue

Tooth nerve

Pulp cavity

Gum

Ligament

Jaw bone

Tooth root

Root canal

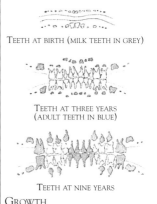

TEETH AT BIRTH (MILK TEETH IN GREY)

TEETH AT THREE YEARS
(ADULT TEETH IN BLUE)

TEETH AT NINE YEARS

THE TEETH
There are three types of teeth: incisors have sharp edges for cutting; canines have pointed tips for tearing; and molars have flattened, ridged surfaces for grinding. Teeth are coated in enamel, the hardest substance in the body. Beneath this is a softer layer of dentine.

GROWTH
All teeth are present at birth as tiny buds deep in the jawbone. The 20 milk teeth usually appear between the ages of six months and three years. The 32 adult teeth usually appear between the ages of six and 20 years.

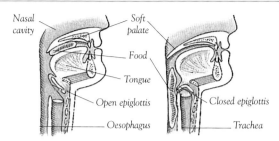

Nasal cavity — Soft palate — Food — Tongue — Open epiglottis — Closed epiglottis — Oesophagus — Trachea

SWALLOWING

When food reaches the back of the mouth, it triggers the swallowing reflex. An automatic wave of muscle contraction propels food through the oesophagus, a muscular tube that leads to the stomach.

MOUTH FACTS

• Some people never develop the back four molars (wisdom teeth).

• Acids, secreted by bacteria in the mouth to break down sugars, cause tooth decay.

• An adult secretes about 1 litre (1.6 pints) of saliva a day.

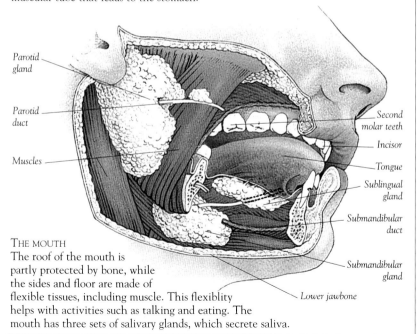

Parotid gland — Parotid duct — Muscles — Second molar teeth — Incisor — Tongue — Sublingual gland — Submandibular duct — Submandibular gland — Lower jawbone

THE MOUTH

The roof of the mouth is partly protected by bone, while the sides and floor are made of flexible tissues, including muscle. This flexiblity helps with activities such as talking and eating. The mouth has three sets of salivary glands, which secrete saliva.

MOUTH AND TEETH

THE STOMACH

WHEN FOOD IS SWALLOWED, it passes down the oesophagus into the stomach, which lies high on the left side of the abdominal cavity. Semi-digested food leaves the stomach through a muscular ring (pyloric sphincter) and enters the intestines.

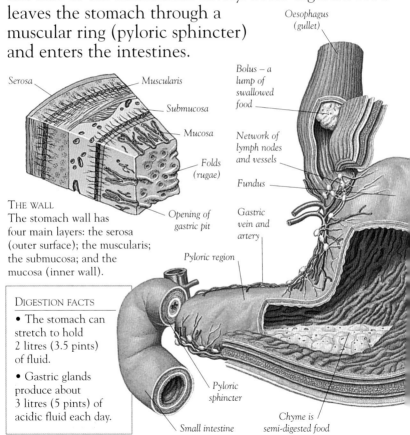

Oesophagus (gullet)

Serosa

Muscularis

Submucosa

Mucosa

Folds (rugae)

Opening of gastric pit

Bolus – a lump of swallowed food

Network of lymph nodes and vessels

Fundus

Gastric vein and artery

Pyloric region

Pyloric sphincter

Small intestine

Chyme is semi-digested food

THE WALL
The stomach wall has four main layers: the serosa (outer surface); the muscularis; the submucosa; and the mucosa (inner wall).

DIGESTION FACTS

• The stomach can stretch to hold 2 litres (3.5 pints) of fluid.

• Gastric glands produce about 3 litres (5 pints) of acidic fluid each day.

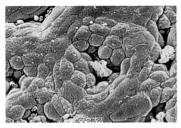

GASTRIC PITS

Glands in the gastric pits secrete hydrochloric acid and powerful enzymes. These break up complex food molecules into simpler chemicals. The stomach does not digest itself because it is protected by a mucus lining.

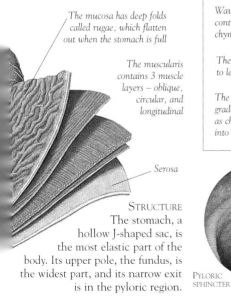

The mucosa has deep folds called rugae, which flatten out when the stomach is full

The muscularis contains 3 muscle layers – oblique, circular, and longitudinal

Serosa

STRUCTURE

The stomach, a hollow J-shaped sac, is the most elastic part of the body. Its upper pole, the fundus, is the widest part, and its narrow exit is in the pyloric region.

FILLING AND EMPTYING

ACTION

Food spends about six hours in the stomach. The muscular wall churns up food ready for digestion. Semi-digested food forms a slurry called chyme.

As food enters, the stomach stretches

More gastric juices are produced

Stomach churning increases and, within a few hours, its contents form chyme

Wave-like muscle contractions push chyme downwards

The pyloric sphincter relaxes to let some chyme through

The stomach gradually shrinks as chyme passes into the duodenum

PYLORIC SPHINCTER

PYLORIC SPHINCTER

This muscular, ring-like thickening of the intestine wall is usually closed to keep the stomach full. It relaxes for a few seconds to let chyme squirt into the intestines.

85

THE INTESTINES

COILED INSIDE the abdominal cavity is the intestinal tube. In the small intestine, nutrients are absorbed and enzymes complete the digestive process. In the large intestine (bowel), wastes are solidified.

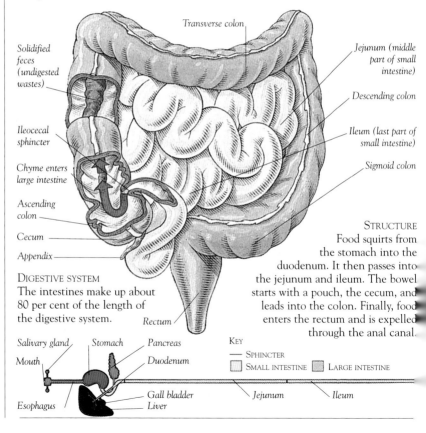

Transverse colon

Solidified feces (undigested wastes)

Ileocecal sphincter

Chyme enters large intestine

Ascending colon

Cecum

Appendix

Jejunum (middle part of small intestine)

Descending colon

Ileum (last part of small intestine)

Sigmoid colon

STRUCTURE
Food squirts from the stomach into the duodenum. It then passes into the jejunum and ileum. The bowel starts with a pouch, the cecum, and leads into the colon. Finally, food enters the rectum and is expelled through the anal canal.

DIGESTIVE SYSTEM
The intestines make up about 80 per cent of the length of the digestive system.

Rectum

Salivary gland

Mouth

Stomach

Pancreas

Duodenum

Esophagus

Gall bladder

Liver

KEY
— SPHINCTER
▢ SMALL INTESTINE ▢ LARGE INTESTINE

Jejunum

Ileum

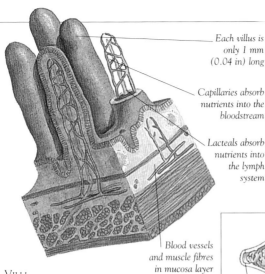

Each villus is only 1 mm (0.04 in) long

Capillaries absorb nutrients into the bloodstream

Lacteals absorb nutrients into the lymph system

Blood vessels and muscle fibres in mucosa layer

INTESTINE FACTS

• The small intestine is about 285 cm (112 in) long.

• The small intestine doubles in length when a person dies.

• The large intestine is about 150 cm (59 in) long.

VILLI
The intestinal wall is covered in tiny projections, called villi. These absorb nutrients from the intestines into the blood capillaries and lymph vessels, called lacteals.

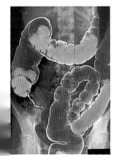

COLON X-RAY
This false-colour X-ray shows part of the large intestine. Here, bacteria break down some fibres and excess water is absorbed. Waste remains soldify to form feces.

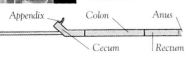

Appendix   Colon   Anus

Cecum   Rectum

Intestine

Food

Muscle contracts behind food

Food slides forward

Muscles in front of food relax

Contractions push food along the digestive tract

PERISTALSIS
The wall of the digestive tract contains longitudinal and circular muscle fibres. These produce wavelike contractions called peristalsis, propelling food through the intestines.

LIVER AND PANCREAS

TWO IMPORTANT ORGANS are closely associated with the intestines: the liver and the pancreas. The liver secretes bile, a digestive juice that breaks down fats and processes nutrients, carried to it from the stomach and intestines by the portal vein. Pancreatic enzymes enter the duodenum to aid digestion.

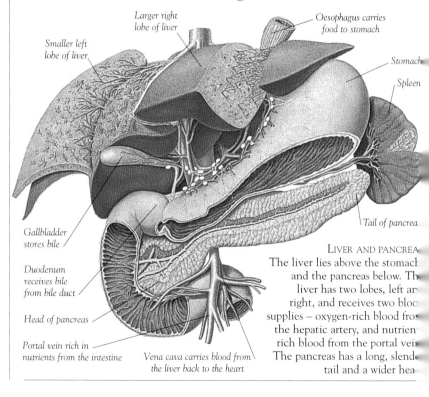

Larger right lobe of liver

Oesophagus carries food to stomach

Smaller left lobe of liver

Stomach

Spleen

Gallbladder stores bile

Duodenum receives bile from bile duct

Head of pancreas

Portal vein rich in nutrients from the intestine

Vena cava carries blood from the liver back to the heart

Tail of pancreas

LIVER AND PANCREAS
The liver lies above the stomach and the pancreas below. The liver has two lobes, left and right, and receives two blood supplies – oxygen-rich blood from the hepatic artery, and nutrient-rich blood from the portal vein. The pancreas has a long, slender tail and a wider head.

LIVER FUNCTIONS

The liver performs many vital functions. It stores chemicals and carries out many different chemical processes.

- Makes bile for digesting food.
- Breaks down fats and excess amino acids (units of protein).
- Helps maintain blood sugar levels.
- Stores fat-soluble vitamins and some minerals (e.g. iron and copper).
- Makes heat to warm passing blood.
- Makes blood proteins.
- Helps clot blood.
- Controls blood cell formation and destruction.
- Removes poisonous chemicals from the blood, and breaks them down.

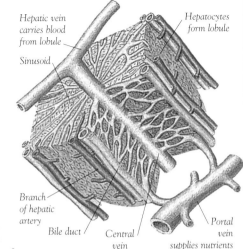

Hepatic vein carries blood from lobule

Sinusoid

Hepatocytes form lobule

Branch of hepatic artery

Bile duct

Central vein

Portal vein supplies nutrients

LIVER LOBULE

Billions of liver cells (hepatocytes) are arranged into thousands of six-sided columns called lobules. Blood flows from both the hepatic artery and portal vein into spaces (sinusoids) to supply oxygen and nutrients to the hepatocytes.

Exocrine glands make digestive enzymes

Ducts carry digestive juices

Endocrine glands secrete hormones into bloodstream

PANCREAS

Some pancreatic cells form clusters of exocrine glands that secrete digestive enzymes. Other pancreatic cells form endocrine glands. These secrete hormones (insulin and glucagon) that help to regulate blood sugar.

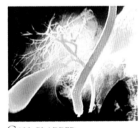

GALL BLADDER

When semi-digested food enters the duodenum, the gallbladder contracts to pump bile through the bile duct into the intestines.

89

URINARY SYSTEM

EXCESS FLUID AND SOLUBLE substances are removed from the blood circulation by the kidneys. Some fluid and nutrients are reabsorbed back into the bloodstream, while excess water and waste products are expelled from the body as urine.

LOCATION OF URINARY SYSTEM

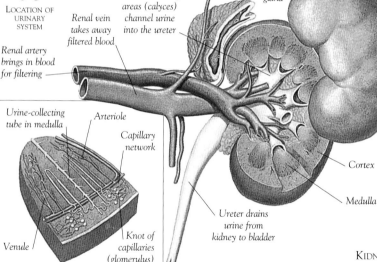

Adrenal gland

Urine-collecting areas (calyces) channel urine into the ureter

Renal vein takes away filtered blood

Renal artery brings in blood for filtering

Cortex

Medulla

Urine-collecting tube in medulla

Arteriole

Capillary network

Venule

Knot of capillaries (glomerulus) in cortex

Ureter drains urine from kidney to bladder

SECTION OF THE KIDNEY
There are over a million filtration units (nephrons); this network of tubules loops down from the cortex to the medulla.

KIDNEYS
The two kidneys are bean-shaped organs at the back of the abdomen. They regulate body-fluid and salt levels and help to control blood acidity. Each kidney is about 12 cm (5 in) long and contains two layers of tissue: an outer cortex and an inner medulla.

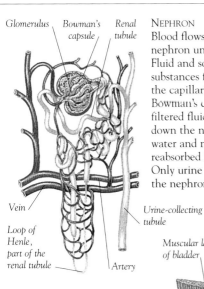

Glomerulus Bowman's Renal
capsule tubule

Vein

Loop of
Henle,
part of the
renal tubule

Artery

Urine-collecting
tubule

NEPHRON

Blood flows into the nephron under pressure. Fluid and soluble substances filter through the capillaries into the Bowman's capsule. As filtered fluid drains down the nephron, most water and nutrients are reabsorbed by the blood. Only urine remains in the nephron.

KIDNEY FACTS

- Every hour, the kidneys filter up to 7 litres (12 pints) of fluid from the blood.

- Urine is 95% water.

- Urine contains poisonous substances including urea, made in the liver.

MALE
URINARY
SYSTEM

Sperm-carrying
tube

Stretchy lining
of bladder

Muscular layer
of bladder

Ureter

URINARY SYSTEM

There are four main stages in the urinary system:

- Kidneys – two organs where fluid and wastes are filtered from blood and concentrated to form urine. This trickles down urine-collecting ducts into the ureters.

- Ureters – two tubes that each run from a kidney to the bladder. Urine constantly trickles down these, day and night.

- Bladder – an elastic sac that stores urine until it can be expelled. The bladder can stretch to hold over half a litre (1 pint) of fluid.

- Urethra – a single tube that drains urine from the bladder to the outside world. The urethra is about 20 cm (8 in) long in men, but only 4 cm (1.5 in) long in women.

Urethra

Bulb of
penis

Prostate
gland

Ischium bone
of pelvis

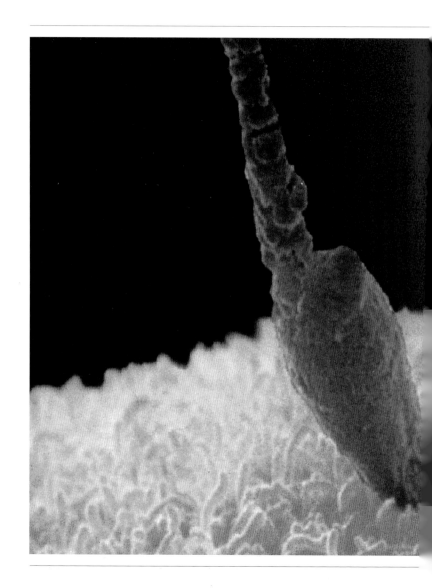

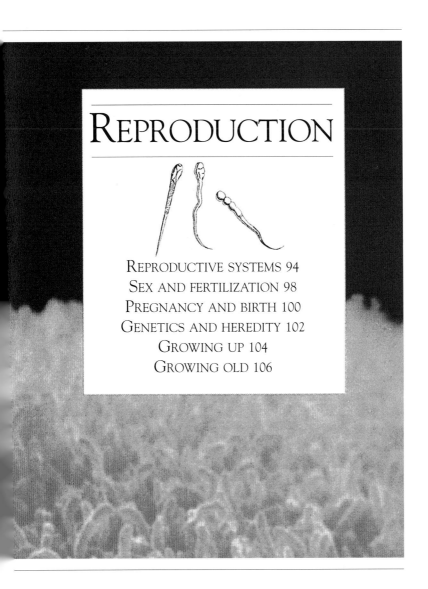

REPRODUCTION

REPRODUCTIVE SYSTEMS

FOR THE HUMAN RACE to continue, people need to reproduce. From the early teens, the male and female reproductive systems produce sex cells. These unite through sexual reproduction to form a new life.

Male reproductive system

The male sex glands are called testes (testicles). These produce mobile sex cells (spermatozoa or sperm). These pass through two tubes, the vas deferens and the epididymis, to reach the penis. Glands, such as the prostate and seminal vesicles, secrete fluids that nourish the sperm.

LOCATION
OF MALE
REPRODUCTIVE
SYSTEM

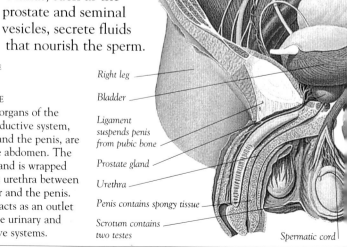

Vena cava   *Aorta*

STRUCTURE

The main organs of the male reproductive system, the testes and the penis, are outside the abdomen. The prostate gland is wrapped around the urethra between the bladder and the penis. The penis acts as an outlet for both the urinary and reproductive systems.

Right leg

Bladder

Ligament suspends penis from pubic bone

Prostate gland

Urethra

Penis contains spongy tissue

Scrotum contains two testes

Spermatic cord

SPERM CELLS

Between an oval head and a whip-like tail is a middle piece, packed with energy-releasing structures called mitochondria. These help the tail propel the sperm along the female reproductive tract. A healthy adult male produces about 500 million sperm a day.

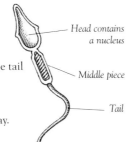

Head contains a nucleus

Middle piece

Tail

SPERM

MALE REPRODUCTION

• A sperm is 0.05 mm (0.002 in) long.

• A sperm takes about 10 weeks to mature.

• Each testis produces about 1,500 sperm per second.

• Sperm swim at a rate of about 3 mm (0.08 in) per hour.

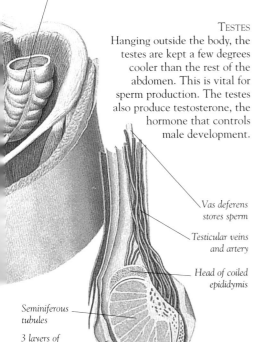

Colon

TESTES

Hanging outside the body, the testes are kept a few degrees cooler than the rest of the abdomen. This is vital for sperm production. The testes also produce testosterone, the hormone that controls male development.

Vas deferens stores sperm

Testicular veins and artery

Head of coiled epididymis

Seminiferous tubules

3 layers of protective tissue

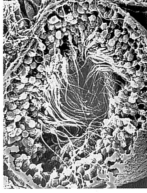

CROSS-SECTION OF TESTIS

DEVELOPING SPERM

The testes contain about 1,000 seminiferous tubules where sperm are produced. They are nourished by special cells, before passing into the tightly coiled epididymis to mature. Here, they are stored until needed.

REPRODUCTIVE SYSTEMS

95

Female reproductive system

The female sex glands are the ovaries. These produce sex cells called ova (eggs). Usually one egg is released every 28 days during the menstrual cycle. It passes down one of two Fallopian tubes into the uterus (womb). If the egg is fertilized by a sperm, it becomes embedded in the womb lining. Otherwise the egg and lining are shed in a menstrual period.

LOCATION OF FEMALE
REPRODUCTIVE SYSTEM

STRUCTURE

The female organs lie in the pelvis. At the lower end of the uterus (womb), a narrow opening (cervix) leads into the vagina. At the top end, two openings lead into the Fallopian tubes. These widen out to embrace the ovaries and trap released eggs.

Ovarian ligament

Uterus has thick wall

Ovary

The Fallopian tube sweeps the released egg down towards the uterus

During the menstrual cycle, several eggs start to ripen, producing bulges on the ovary surface. Usually only one egg is released

The vagina has a muscular wall that stretches during childbirth

The womb lining plumps up each month, ready to receive the fertilized egg

UTERUS

Normally about the size of a fist, the uterus is a pear-shaped organ with a thick, muscular wall. During pregnancy it can expand over a 1,000 times in volume to hold a developing baby.

The ovum (egg)

In the ovary, ova ripen in fluid-filled follicles. Once a month, one follicle outgrows the others and bursts, releasing its egg. An ovum is surrounded by follicle cells and a membrane (zona pellucida).

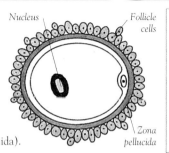

Nucleus

Follicle cells

Zona pellucida

The menstrual cycle

The menstrual cycle is controlled by the pituitary gland. This produces hormones that stimulate the ovaries to produce oestrogen and progesterone, and trigger the release of an egg. At the same time, the womb lining undergoes cyclical changes.

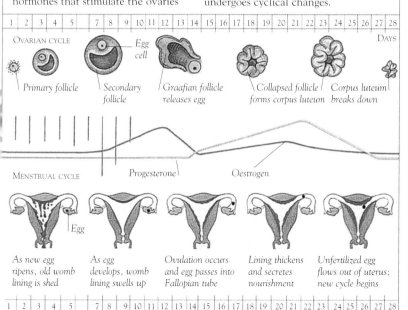

| 1 | 2 | 3 | 4 | 5 | | 7 | 8 | 9 | 10 | 11 | 12 | 13 | 14 | 15 | 16 | 17 | 18 | 19 | 20 | 21 | 22 | 23 | 24 | 25 | 26 | 27 | 28 |

Ovarian cycle

Egg cell

DAYS

Primary follicle

Secondary follicle

Graafian follicle releases egg

Collapsed follicle forms corpus luteum

Corpus luteum breaks down

Progesterone

Oestrogen

Menstrual cycle

Egg

As new egg ripens, old womb lining is shed

As egg develops, womb lining swells up

Ovulation occurs and egg passes into Fallopian tube

Lining thickens and secretes nourishment

Unfertilized egg flows out of uterus; new cycle begins

| 1 | 2 | 3 | 4 | 5 | | 7 | 8 | 9 | 10 | 11 | 12 | 13 | 14 | 15 | 16 | 17 | 18 | 19 | 20 | 21 | 22 | 23 | 24 | 25 | 26 | 27 | 28 |

REPRODUCTIVE SYSTEMS

SEX AND FERTILIZATION

SPERM CELLS ENTER the female's body during sexual
intercourse; if a sperm fertilizes an egg, new life begins.
The sperm and the ovum contain genetic material,
which is joined through sexual reproduction to
provide instructions for the development of the baby.

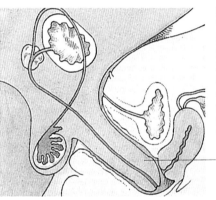

SEXUAL INTERCOURSE
The male's penis fills with blood and
becomes hard and erect. It is inserted
into the woman's vagina. Sexual
intercourse can produce pleasurable
sensations for both partners. In the
male, reflex contractions suddenly
release (ejaculate) a fluid (semen)
containing sperm into the
woman's vagina.

*The penis is placed
inside the vagina*

*Millions of sperm race
towards the ripe egg*

FERTILIZATION FACTS

• A newly released
egg must be fertilized
within 24–48 hours.

• A baby is usually
born about 40 weeks
after fertilization.

• Sometimes a newly
fertilized egg splits to
produce identical twins.

SPERM RACE
A man's semen
usually contains
about 300 million
sperm. These swim
in search of an egg.
Only 50–150 sperm
reach the egg as it
travels down a
Fallopian tube. Of
these, only one will
fertilize the egg.

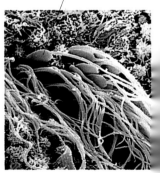

SPERM SWIMMING IN SEMEN

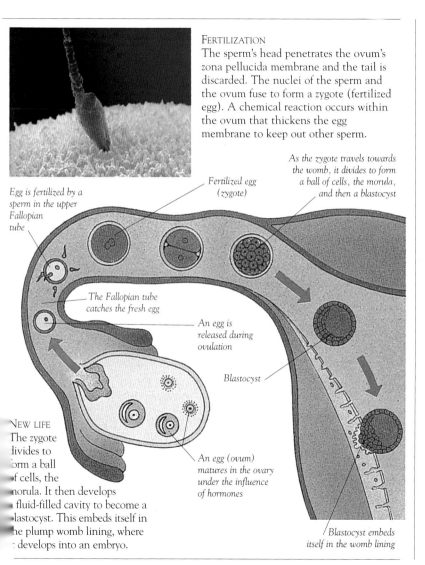

FERTILIZATION
The sperm's head penetrates the ovum's zona pellucida membrane and the tail is discarded. The nuclei of the sperm and the ovum fuse to form a zygote (fertilized egg). A chemical reaction occurs within the ovum that thickens the egg membrane to keep out other sperm.

As the zygote travels towards the womb, it divides to form a ball of cells, the morula, and then a blastocyst

Fertilized egg (zygote)

Egg is fertilized by a sperm in the upper Fallopian tube

The Fallopian tube catches the fresh egg

An egg is released during ovulation

Blastocyst

NEW LIFE
The zygote divides to form a ball of cells, the morula. It then develops a fluid-filled cavity to become a blastocyst. This embeds itself in the plump womb lining, where it develops into an embryo.

An egg (ovum) matures in the ovary under the influence of hormones

Blastocyst embeds itself in the womb lining

99

PREGNANCY AND BIRTH

DURING THE FIRST EIGHT weeks of pregnancy, while the internal organs are developing, the baby is called an embryo. Once movement begins and the organs have formed, it is known as a fetus. Growth is then rapid.

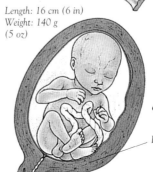

8 WEEKS
The fetus is protected by amniotic fluid and is nourished through the umbilical cord.

Length: 2.5 cm (1 in)
Weight: 2 g (0.07 oz)

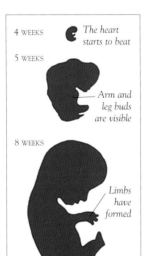

4 WEEKS   The heart starts to beat

5 WEEKS
Arm and leg buds are visible

8 WEEKS
Limbs have formed

THE EMBRYO
These pictures show the actual size of an embryo as it becomes recognizably human in shape.

12 WEEKS
The head is large compared with the body. Tiny nails grow on the fingers and toes. The eyes are closed. 32 permanent teeth buds develop.

Length: 16 cm (6 in)
Weight: 140 g (5 oz)

Length: 7.5 cm (3 in)
Weight: 18 g (0.6 oz)

16 WEEKS
The fetus is covered in fine, downy hair. External genitals are visible. Movement can sometimes be felt from 16 weeks.

Placenta supplies fetus with nutrients and oxygen, and removes fetal waste

100

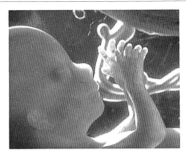

FETUS AT FOUR MONTHS

THE FETUS

The umbilical cord connects the fetus to the placenta, a spongy organ attached to the womb lining. By 16 weeks, the facial features are well formed and blood vessels are visible under the paper-thin skin.

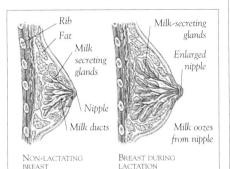

NON-LACTATING BREAST

BREAST DURING LACTATION

LACTATION

During pregnancy, the breasts enlarge, and milk glands develop. Breast milk provides nourishment and protective antibodies for the newborn child.

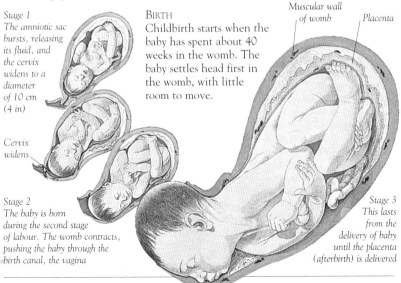

Stage 1
The amniotic sac bursts, releasing its fluid, and the cervix widens to a diameter of 10 cm (4 in)

Cervix widens

BIRTH

Childbirth starts when the baby has spent about 40 weeks in the womb. The baby settles head first in the womb, with little room to move.

Muscular wall of womb

Placenta

Stage 2
The baby is born during the second stage of labour. The womb contracts, pushing the baby through the birth canal, the vagina

Stage 3
This lasts from the delivery of baby until the placenta (afterbirth) is delivered

GENETICS AND HEREDITY

FOUND IN THE NUCLEUS of each cell are structures called chromosomes. These contain molecules of deoxyribonucleic acid (DNA), which are made up of strings of genes. Each gene unit contains the information needed to make a single protein used to build and control cells. Genes decide a person's characteristics, such as hair and eye colour. Through sexual reproduction, sex cells pass genes onto the next generation.

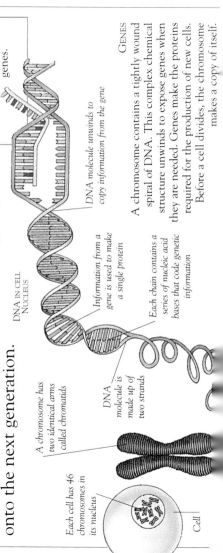

GENETICS FACTS

- Sperm have an X or a Y chromosome that determines a baby's sex.
- The majority of body cells contain 46 chromosomes.
- Red blood cells have no nucleus and so do not carry genes.

DNA IN CELL NUCLEUS

Information from a gene is used to make a single protein

Each chain contains a series of nucleic acid bases that code genetic information

A chromosome has two identical arms called chromatids

DNA molecule is made up of two strands

DNA molecule unwinds to copy information from the gene

GENES

A chromosome contains a tightly wound spiral of DNA. This complex chemical structure unwinds to expose genes when they are needed. Genes make the proteins required for the production of new cells. Before a cell divides, the chromosome makes a copy of itself.

Each cell has 46 chromosomes in its nucleus

Cell

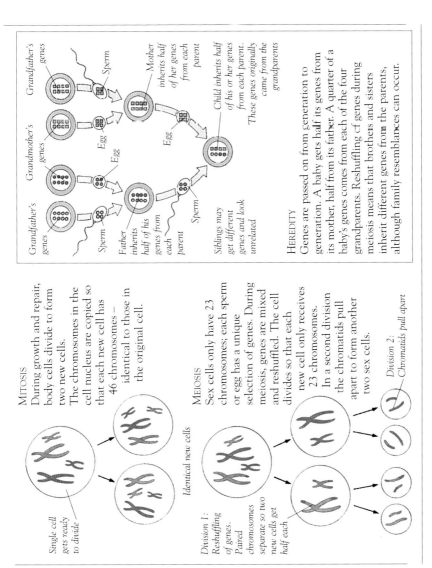

MITOSIS

During growth and repair, body cells divide to form two new cells.

The chromosomes in the cell nucleus are copied so that each new cell has 46 chromosomes – identical to those in the original cell.

Single cell gets ready to divide

Identical new cells

MEIOSIS

Sex cells only have 23 chromosomes; each sperm or egg has a unique selection of genes. During meiosis, genes are mixed and reshuffled. The cell divides so that each new cell only receives 23 chromosomes.

In a second division the chromatids pull apart to form another two sex cells.

Division 1: Reshuffling of genes. Paired chromosomes separate so two new cells get half each

Division 2: Chromatids pull apart

Grandfather's genes

Grandmother's genes

Grandmother's genes

Grandfather's genes

Sperm

Egg

Egg

Mother inherits half of her genes from each parent

Sperm

Egg

Father inherits half of his genes from each parent

Sperm

Child inherits half of his or her genes from each parent. These genes originally came from the grandparents

Siblings may get different genes and look unrelated

HEREDITY

Genes are passed on from generation to generation. A baby gets half its genes from its mother, half from its father. A quarter of a baby's genes comes from each of the four grandparents. Reshuffling of genes during meiosis means that brothers and sisters inherit different genes from the parents, although family resemblances can occur.

GENETICS AND HEREDITY

GROWING UP

GROWTH IS RAPID during the first few years of life, when children learn to walk and talk. It steadies during childhood, and then speeds up again at puberty, when psychological and physical changes occur that make reproduction possible. By the late teens, growth stops and adulthood begins.

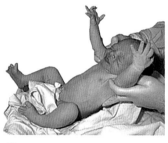

HELPLESS BABY
A newborn baby can hear well but cannot see properly. It may spend at least 12 hours each day asleep. The only way a baby can show fear, discomfort, pain, hunger, or boredom is by crying.

BODY PROPORTIONS
During growth and development, physical proportions change dramatically so that the head becomes smaller in relation to the body.

• A baby's head is about a quarter of total body length.

• During childhood, the relative size of the head and trunk decreases while the legs and arms become proportionately longer.

• An adult's head is about an eighth of total body length.

• A newborn baby can grow from a length of about 51 cm (20 in) to an eventual height of 180 cm (6 ft) or more.

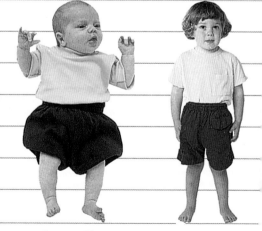

2 MONTHS: 55 CM
(1FT 10 IN)

2 YEARS: 86 CM
(2FT 10 IN)

CHILD DEVELOPMENT

6 MONTHS
Babies can sit up if supported and control the weight of their head.

9–12 MONTHS
Most babies can crawl and pull themselves upright. They may be able to stand without support.

18 MONTHS
Children can walk unaided, climb stairs, and know at least six words.

2–3 YEARS
Children can hold a pencil, scribble, and copy simple shapes. They talk in simple sentences.

PUBERTY FACTS

• During puberty, people become sexually mature; eggs or sperm start being produced.

• Puberty is triggered by hormones released from the brain.

• In girls, puberty starts between the ages of 9–13. In boys, puberty starts later, between the ages of 10–14.

• Hormonal changes at puberty often cause greasy skin and acne.

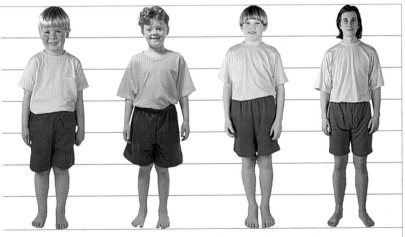

4 YEARS: 112 CM
(3 FT 8 IN)

7 YEARS: 122 CM
(4 FT)

12 YEARS: 147 CM
(4 FT 10 IN)

20 YEARS: 178 CM
(5 FT 10 IN)

GROWING UP

GROWING OLD

AS PEOPLE GROW OLDER, their body cells gradually deteriorate. This results in physical changes such as brittle bones. Medical advances have increased the average life span, lengthening the aging period. A good diet and regular exercise can delay the signs of aging.

AGING
Typical signs of aging include wrinkles and grey or white hair. Wrinkles first appear on the forehead, where skin is creased from smiling and frowning.

EFFECTS OF AGE ON THE REPRODUCTIVE SYSTEMS

Men make sperm and remain fertile from puberty throughout the rest of their lives. Women run out of eggs at an average age of 51 years, when they go through menopause. The ovarian and menstrual cycles cease; at this time a woman is no longer naturally fertile.

MEN

• From the age of 45, a man's prostate gland naturally enlarges and may interfere with his urine flow.

• Men can still father a child at the age of 90 or older.

WOMEN

• Many women suffer menopausal symptoms such as hot flushes, sweating, and mood changes when the ovaries stop making the hormone oestrogen.

• Lack of oestrogen can trigger brittleness in bones and quicken the hardening of the arteries. Hormone replacement therapy can help to prevent these problems and relieve menopausal symptoms.

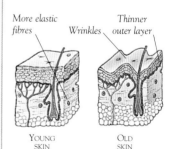

More elastic fibres   *Wrinkles*   *Thinner outer layer*

YOUNG SKIN   OLD SKIN

SKIN
With age, skin becomes tougher, less elastic, and wrinkly. The cells of the outer layer are renewed less often, and the deeper layers lose many of their supporting tissues.

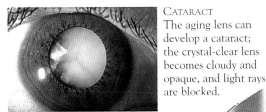

CATARACT

An operation can remove a cataract

CATARACT
The aging lens can develop a cataract; the crystal-clear lens becomes cloudy and opaque, and light rays are blocked.

VISION
As people grow older, the lens of the eye often stiffens and cannot focus on nearby objects. This causes long-sightedness. The retina's macula, where fine detail is picked out, may degenerate so that eyesight begins to fail.

Lens loses elasticity and cannot focus

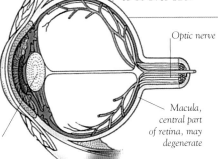

Optic nerve

Macula, central part of retina, may degenerate

ARTERIES
Aging arteries lose their elasticity. Damage due to smoking, high blood pressure, or eating excess fat causes arteries to harden and clog up with fatty deposits. Blood clots may form and block the circulation.

Lining of artery   Build-up of fatty deposits

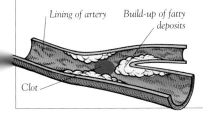

Clot

COMMON CAUSES OF DEATH

The elderly often die peacefully in their sleep, when their heart stops beating.

CAUSE	WHAT HAPPENS?
Heart attack	Heart stops beating due to poor blood supply and lack of oxygen.
Stroke	Brain cells die suddenly due to blockage of a major blood vessel.
Cancer	Uncontrollable growth of abnormal cells causes weakness.
Broncho-pneumonia	Overwhelming airway infection interferes with breathing.
Accident	Injury to a vital organ or loss of blood produces collapse.

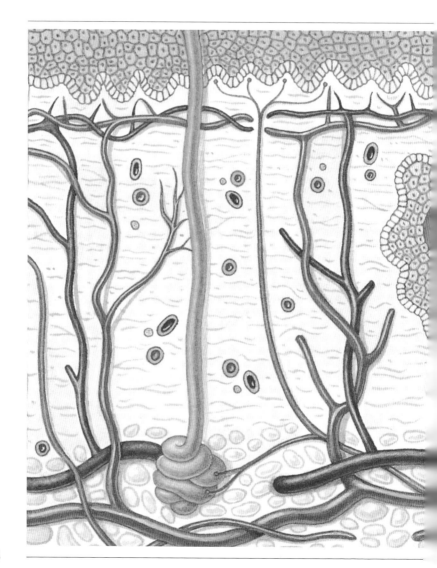

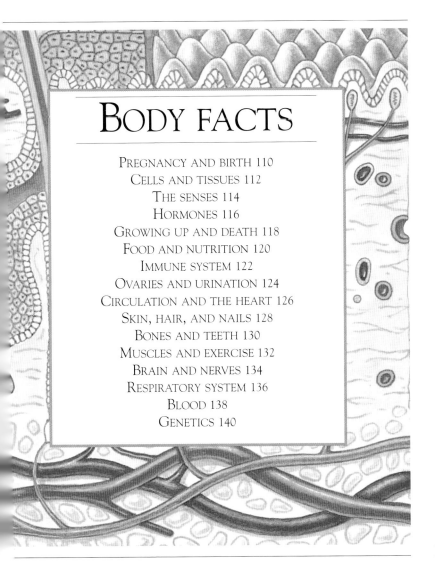

BODY FACTS

CELL FACTS

- There are about 10 billion cells in the human body.

- There are over 200 different kinds of cells including nerve cells, skin cells, blood cells and fat cells.

- Most cells only live for a fairly short time and are continually being replaced by new cells.

- Some cells can regenerate when they are damaged, such as those that make up the skin.

- Nerve cells live for a long time and are not replaced after they die.

- Cells are so small, that around 40 of them would fit on to a full stop.

- Red cells do not have a nucleus.

CELL MEMBRANE

A cell is like a tiny, fluid-filled, squashy bag. The cell is held together by a thin, flexible layer called a plasma membrane. The membrane allows some chemicals to pass through it, while keeping out others.

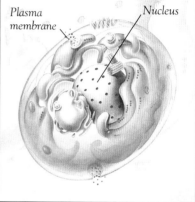

Plasma membrane

Nucleus

TAKING SAMPLES OF CELLS

- In a cervical smear test, some cells are scraped off the cervix with a spatula and then examined under a microscope.

- Cells may be taken from a solid lump, such as a breast lump, using a needle and syringe.

- A urine sample spun in a centrifuge will separate into liquid and cells.

- Blood can also be centrifuged, to provide information about the number of white cells, red cells and platelets (cells used in blood clotting) that are present.

- Fluid removed from around the spinal cord contains cells. Analysis of this fluid can help to identify some serious infections.

TAKING SAMPLES OF TISSUES

- A tissue sample may be taken from the body to diagnose an illness or other medical condition.

- Tissue samples are taken only when less invasive tests are inadequate.

- A piece of tissue may be cut out completely, such as in a skin biopsy.

- A core of tissue can be removed using a specially designed instrument. This is used for a brain biopsy.

- After an entire organ is removed, part of the tissue may be examined microscopically.

- A tissue sample is stored, often in formalin (a preservative) and then thinly sliced for analysis.

- Specially formulated dyes are used to highlight different structures within cells and tissues. These can then be identified more easily when viewed under a microscope.

LIVER BIOPSY

In a liver biopsy, the patient is given a local anaesthetic and a hollow needle is inserted into the liver through a small incision between the right lower ribs. A sample is collected and sent to a laboratory for microscopic examination. This procedure is used to diagnose conditions such as cancer, cirrhosis and hepatitis.

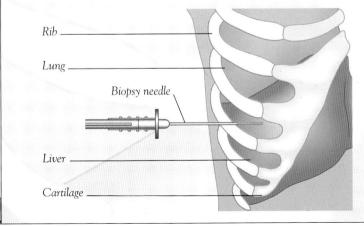

Rib

Lung

Biopsy needle

Liver

Cartilage

PREGNANCY AND BIRTH

PHYSICAL CHANGES DURING PREGNANCY

- Most of the weight gained in pregnancy is in the form of fat.

- The breasts enlarge as milk-producing glands in them multiply in preparation for breast-feeding.

- It is normal for the area around the nipples – the areola – to darken and enlarge.

- The enlarging womb can be felt just above the pubic bone by 12 weeks.

- About half way through the pregnancy, the top of the womb reaches the woman's navel.

- By eight months, the womb cannot grow upwards any further, so the woman's waistline grows outwards.

- Late in pregnancy, a dark line appears on the skin from the navel to the pubic bone.

- This line is called the linea nigra.

THE DEVELOPING FETUS

- A normal pregnancy lasts 40 weeks, counting from the first day of the woman's last period.

- The heart begins to beat before the fetus is a month old. By eight weeks, the fetus has all of its organs, arms and legs.

- The eyelids remain fused shut from weeks 9-10 until week 26. Eyebrows are well developed by 20 weeks.

- The fingernails appear in weeks 9-12, and by week 14 they are well formed.

- The mother will start to feel the fetus moving from weeks 16-20 onwards.

- After 32 weeks, the fetal lungs produce a detergent called surfactant, which makes it possible to breathe without assistance.

- In the final weeks inside the womb, the fetus gains approximately 14 g (0.5 oz) of fat each day.

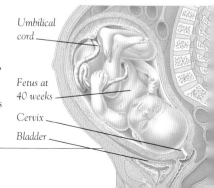

Umbilical cord

Fetus at 40 weeks

Cervix

Bladder

IDENTICAL TWINS

In the uterus, the fetus is protected by a fluid-filled bag known as the amniotic sac. Nourishment is provided by the placenta. Identical twins may share either or both of these. This illustration shows identical twins sharing a placenta.

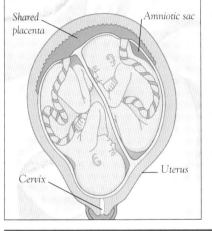

Shared placenta

Amniotic sac

Cervix

Uterus

TYPES OF BIRTH

- In a normal birth, the baby is squeezed through the neck of the womb and out of the vagina.

- Most babies are born head first. Around 3% of babies are born bottom first – this is a breech birth.

- Under Roman law, the fetus had to be taken from the body of a dying mother during pregnancy or labour – the original Caesarean section. Contrary to popular myth, Julius Caesar was not born this way.

- Caesarean section is ten times more dangerous than a normal delivery

- In most cases, a baby is born with the top of the head coming out first and facing towards the back. Around 1 in every 300 babies is born facing toward the front.

TWINS AND MULTIPLE BIRTHS

- Non-identical twins occur when two eggs are fertilized by two sperm.

- Identical twins develop from a single egg fertilized by a single sperm, but which has split early in development.

- Non-identical twins are more common in families with twins, or in couples undergoing fertility treatment.

- Identical twins occur around three times in every 1,000 pregnancies.

- Triplets are born around once in every 6,000 births; quadruplets about once in every 500,000.

- Siamese (conjoined) twins are named after Chang and Eng, born in Siam (Thailand) in 1811.

EYES AND SEEING

- Most of the eye's focusing power is provided by the cornea – the transparent central part covering the iris. The lens provides fine focus control.

- The retina – the light-sensitive layer at the back of the eyeball – contains about 106 million cells.

- Most of the cells on the retina are known as rods. They detect black, white and low-intensity light. The cone cells detect colour.

- Each eye gives a slightly different view of the world. The brain combines these views to provide a three-dimensional image.

EYEBALL

The human eye is a tough ball filled with a fluid that sits in a bony socket. The cornea protects the eye and focuses light. The iris controls the amount of light passing through the pupil to the retina, which sends signals to the brain via the optic nerve.

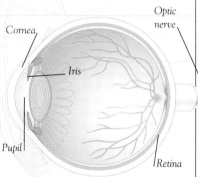

Cornea

Optic nerve

Iris

Pupil

Retina

EYE CHANGES WITH AGE

- Most infants are long-sighted, but this lessens as they grow. This is known as emmetropization. Near-sightedness often becomes apparent in adolescence.

- With age, people may need reading glasses as lenses in the eyes become less able to change shape. This is known as presbyobia.

- Half of all people over 80 have cataracts, usually in both eyes.

- The gradual deterioration of rod cells with age makes vision in low light more difficult.

- Age-related degeneration of the eyes is the most common form of blindness or loss of vision in developed countries.

114

TESTING HEARING

- An audiometer emits pure tone signals to test hearing ability. The test takes place in a sound-proofed room.

- A baby's hearing is tested using an otoacoustic emission test. This detects an echo from the inner ear in response to a sound.

- Tympanometry provides detailed information about the eardrum and bones of the middle ear in response to sound.

- Weber's test uses a vibrating tuning fork placed on the forehead. Normally the sound is heard equally in both ears.

- In Rinne's test, a vibrating tuning fork is placed in front of and then behind each ear. The sound is usually heard loudest behind the ear.

TASTE AND SMELL

- Human beings can detect between 10,000-40,000 different smells using around 20 million smell cells.

- After a while, what seemed like a powerful smell becomes less apparent. This is called habituation.

- Your sense of taste is created by about 100,000 taste buds on your tongue, as well as the inside of your mouth and throat.

- Four taste types (sweet, salty, sour and bitter) combine with the texture, appearance and smell of your food when you eat.

- Sensitivity to taste decreases with age. Elderly people have about half the taste ability of babies, so some food can taste bland to them.

PUPIL SIZE

Your pupils dilate (enlarge) in low light levels, as well as when you are scared or aroused. They constrict (get smaller) in bright light or when you are working on something close up. Two sets of muscles in the iris control the changes in pupil size. To make the pupil constrict, the circular muscles contract (tighten up). The radial muscles contract to make the pupil dilate.

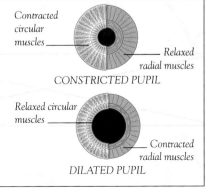

Contracted circular muscles

Relaxed radial muscles

CONSTRICTED PUPIL

Relaxed circular muscles

Contracted radial muscles

DILATED PUPIL

HORMONES

Hormones are chemicals made and stored in glands and then transported in the blood to act on various parts of the body. Hormones control many aspects of normal body processes, including growth and energy levels and the level of glucose in blood.

PARATHYROID GLANDS

- There are four parathyroid glands, each measuring about 5 mm (0.2 in) in diameter, lying to either side of and behind the thyroid gland.

- These small glands regulate the levels of the chemicals calcium and phosphorus in your body.

- A low calcium level in the blood stimulates production of parathyroid hormones, and a high level of calcium does the opposite.

- Parathyroid hormones increase the calcium levels in your body:

  1 Making your bones release calcium directly into the blood stream.

  2 Activating vitamin D, which, in turn, makes your intestine absorb more calcium from the food that you have eaten.

  3 Reducing the amount of calcium that your kidneys excrete in your urine.

FEEDBACK MECHANISM

In order to maintain correct levels of substances in the blood, the secretion (release) of hormones is regulated by feedback mechanisms. This illustration shows how the parathyroid glands detect changes in calcium levels in the blood and then secrete appropriate amounts of parathyroid hormone (PTH) to correct them. All of the glands in the body work in much the same way.

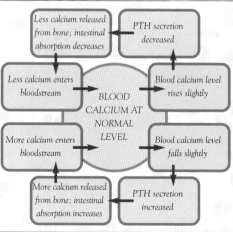

Less calcium released from bone; intestinal absorption decreases

PTH secretion decreased

Less calcium enters bloodstream

BLOOD CALCIUM AT NORMAL LEVEL

Blood calcium level rises slightly

More calcium enters bloodstream

Blood calcium level falls slightly

More calcium released from bone; intestinal absorption increases

PTH secretion increased

THE THYROID GLAND

- Women have larger thyroid glands than men. In some women, the thyroid gland enlarges during menstruation.

- Weighing around 30 g (1 oz), the gland is wrapped around the windpipe in the lower part of your neck.

- The thyroid gland moves up and down when you swallow.

- Thyroid hormones help to control your energy levels.

- The thyroid gland is controlled by the pituitary gland in the brain.

- Iodine is essential for the formation of thyroid hormone.

- Thyroid hormones are essential for normal growth.

ADRENALINE

Adrenaline has the following actions:

- The liver and muscles release glucose to provide an extra source of energy.

- Fat tissue is broken down to produce additional energy.

- Muscles develop greater endurance and so tire less easily.

- The heart contracts more forcibly and beats much faster.

WHEN ARE HORMONES PRODUCED?

- Levels of prolactin (a hormone used in the production of milk in women) and of growth hormones increase during sleep.

- Follicle stimulating hormone and luteinising hormone are important for a woman's menstrual system and a man's testicles. They are released in pulses, every two hours or so.

- Levels of cortisol, which helps to control the body's metabolism are highest in the early morning and lowest overnight.

- Adrenaline, cortisol, growth hormone and prolactin are all produced when the body is stressed.

Adrenaline is produced when the body is stressed.

BODY FACTS

GROWTH CHARTS FOR CHILDREN

Growth charts are used to record a child's growth from 2 to 18 years. To measure your child's height, ask the child to stand up straight with his or her back against a wall or door. Lower a book on to your child's head and mark where the base of the book meets the wall. Your child's growth curve can be compared with the typical range, shown by the shaded part of the graph.

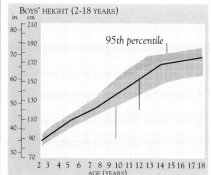

BOYS' HEIGHT (2-18 YEARS)

95th percentile

AGE (YEARS)

Boys will not reach their full height until about 16-18 years of age. There will be a brief growth spurt at the time of puberty which usually occurs between the ages of 12 and 14. The top of the shaded area represents the 95th percentile. Below this line sits 95 percent of the population.

Because girls tend to reach puberty before boys, they will arrive at their maximum height by about the ages of 14-16. Similarly, any growth spurt will occur a few years earlier, around the ages of 10 and 12. The bottom of the shaded area represents the 5th percentile. Only 5 percent of children will fall below this line.

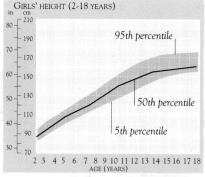

GIRLS' HEIGHT (2-18 YEARS)

95th percentile

50th percentile

5th percentile

AGE (YEARS)

WORLDWIDE CAUSES OF DEATH

In 1999, there were 52 million deaths worldwide. The top 10 leading causes of death were as follows:

1 Heart disease – 14%.

2 Cerebrovascular disease – 9.5%.

3 Acute lower respiratory tract infections – 6.4%.

4 HIV and AIDS – 4.2%.

5 Obstructed airways disease – 4.2% .

6 Diarrhoeal diseases – 4.1%.

7 Problems at birth – 4.0%.

8 Tuberculosis – 2.8%.

9 Lung cancer – 2.3%.

10 Road traffic accidents – 2.2%.

HEALTHY LIVING FOR LONGEVITY

Medical evidence indicates that the following lifestyle habits increase everyone's chances of living a long and healthy life:

• No tobacco smoking.

• Alcohol in moderation.

• Regular aerobic exercise.

• Healthy eating.

• Regular health screening, including blood pressure measurement and cancer checks.

• Women should be screened regularly for breast and cervical cancers.

• Preventing complications in established diseases, such as taking aspirin for heart disease.

BODY CHANGES IN A LIFETIME

• At birth, the heart beats 120-160 times every minute. In adulthood, it slows to 60-80 times a minute.

• The breathing rate is 30-50 breaths per minute at birth, slowing to around 15 per minute by adulthood.

• Elderly kidneys take longer to work, so chemicals may accumulate that would normally be excreted.

• Children's bones are two-thirds cartilage. By the age of 18, this all is replaced by solid bone.

• Children's kidneys cannot make urine as concentrated as an adult's.

• At the age of 18, all the nerve cells are connected. By the time a person reaches 90, the brain has lost one-tenth of its tissue.

EATING AND DIGESTING

- 10 French fries provide the same amount of energy as six tomatoes, or eight cups of sliced mushrooms.

- It would take a person who weighed 68 kg (150lb) approximately 1.5 hours to walk off all of the calories contained within the average T-bone steak.

- Food stays in the stomach for two to four hours.

- Food usually spends at least 10 hours in the large intestine. It can be there for up to several days.

- Some people may have a bowel movement several times a day; some only twice a week. Both levels of activity are normal.

- About 75% of faeces is made up of water. The rest is mainly undigested plant fibres and germs.

HUNGER AND APPETITE

When the body needs food, or at times of the day when it expects a routine meal, the nervous and hormonal systems cause the stomach to contract, resulting in the sensation of hunger. Appetite is caused by the production of digestive juices in the mouth and stomach.

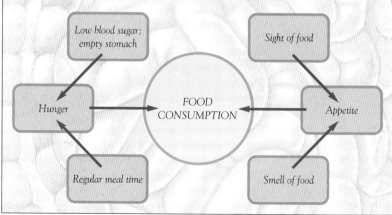

FAT FACTS

- Fats should make up no more than 30% of the calories in a diet.

- Vitamins A, D, E and K are found in fatty foods and are essential for your health.

- The body makes its own cholesterol in the liver. It plays an essential role in stabilizing the body's cells.

- Cholesterol levels are influenced by the total amount of fat in your diet. If it builds up in the arteries, it can contribute to a heart attack.

- Animal fat, which is high in saturated fats, is the main cause of a high cholesterol level.

- Transfats in butter substitutes and some processed food also increase levels of cholesterol.

- People living in Mediterranean countries consume large amounts of monounsaturated fat, as found in olive oil. These people tend to have low levels of heart disease.

Fast foods, such as burgers, tend to contain large amounts of fat.

MINERALS

- The major minerals are calcium, chloride, magnesium, phosphorus, potassium, sodium and sulphur.

- A healthy diet should contain sufficient minerals without the need to take supplements.

- Three-quarters of the mineral content of the body is made up of calcium and phosphorus and is found in the bones the skeleton.

- Over half of the body's magnesium is found in the bones.

ENERGY AND WEIGHT LOSS

- The rate at which energy is used is known as the basal metabolic rate.

- To lose weight you have to expend more energy than you eat.

- The metabolic rate is higher in children than in adults. Therefore, if you eat the same amount of food throughout your life, you will increase your weight.

- The taller you are, the greater your metabolic rate.

IMMUNE SYSTEM

ANTIBODIES

Antibodies are substances in the blood that destroy or neutralise various harmful poisons as well as infections caused by bacteria.

- Antibodies are made by a type of white cell known as a b lymphocyte.

- G antibodies can transfer across the placenta to provide protection in babies in the womb.

- A antibodies are commonly found in secretions and colostrum (breast milk produced for the first few days after birth).

- E antibodies are produced in response to allergic reactions.

- M antibodies are the first to be produced after an infection.

- Autoantibodies attack the body's own organs and can produce autoimmune disease.

Viruses can be carried in the droplets of a sneeze.

INFECTIONS

These are some of the ways in which different infections are spread from person to person:

- Millions of virus particles are transported through the air in the droplets of a sneeze.

- Some infections, such as herpes, are spread by touching the infected area.

- By not washing your hands after going to the toilet and before eating, you can consume some infections such as toxoplasmosis.

- Some serious infections, such as HIV, are transmitted by sharing infected hypodermic needles.

- Many diseases are transmitted during sexual intercourse, including hepatitis B, syphilis and gonorrhoea.

- Insects can transmit infection. Malaria, for example, is carried by infected mosquitoes.

- Immunization against diseases helps to prevent the spread of infections.

- Some viruses, such as influenza, are continually changing, so a new vaccine has to be administered every year to maintain immunity.

NATURAL BARRIERS AGAINST INFECTION

- The lining of the respiratory tract contains little hairs, which trap dust particles.

- Glands in the stomach produce hydrochloric acid, which destroys bacteria.

- Tears are produced to help to wash away dirt and germs from the eyes.

- Saliva contains a mixture of mucus and enzymes that clean the mouth.

- The skin is protected by an oily substance called sebum.

- Harmless bacteria in the genital tract help to prevent the growth of more harmful bacteria. Urination flushes out organisms from the bladder.

THE INFLAMMATORY RESPONSE

If foreign organisms, such as bacteria, overcome the body's primary physical and chemical barriers, the next line of defence is the inflammatory response. This is characterized by redness, pain, heat and swelling at the damaged area.

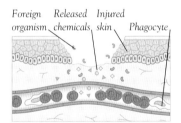

Foreign organism *Released chemicals* *Injured skin* *Phagocyte*

1 Foreign organisms invade the body through skin that has been broken due to injury. Instantly, the damaged tissue releases specific chemicals that attract specialized white blood cells called phagocytes.

2 The chemicals cause the underlying blood vessel to widen and the flow of blood to increase, leading to the symptoms of inflammation. The vessel walls become slightly porous, allowing phagocytes to reach, engulf and destroy the foreign organisms.

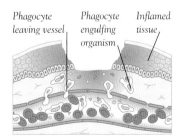

Phagocyte leaving vessel *Phagocyte engulfing organism* *Inflamed tissue*

THE OVARIES

- At birth, a girl's ovaries contain around 2-4 million eggs. No more are produced after birth.

- Each month, around 20 eggs develop in little sacs called follicles in the ovaries. Only one egg is released – this is known as ovulation.

- Only around 400 eggs will be ovulated. The others degenerate.

- Ovulation usually occurs 14 days before the first day of a woman's period.

- Ovulation tends to alternate between the ovaries, at monthly intervals. A month when no egg is produced is known as an anovulatory cycle.

- At ovulation there may be some pain and a small amount of bleeding – known as Mittleschmurtz.

- At the menopause, eggs stop maturing and are no longer released each month.

- The ovaries produce the hormones oestrogen and progesterone.

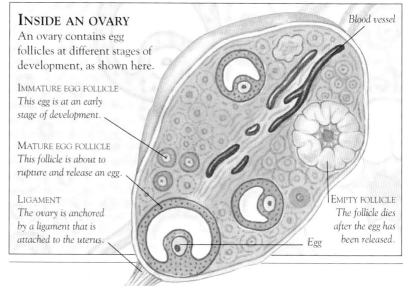

INSIDE AN OVARY
An ovary contains egg follicles at different stages of development, as shown here.

IMMATURE EGG FOLLICLE
This egg is at an early stage of development.

MATURE EGG FOLLICLE
This follicle is about to rupture and release an egg.

LIGAMENT
The ovary is anchored by a ligament that is attached to the uterus.

Blood vessel

EMPTY FOLLICLE
The follicle dies after the egg has been released.

Egg

URINATION AND THE BLADDER

- The medical word for passing urine is "micturition".

- Urine arrives at the bladder via two muscular tubes called ureters.

- The bladder is made of a muscle tissue known as detrusor muscle.

- As the bladder fills, it stretches, sending a signal to the brain to go to the toilet.

- It is possible to override this signal until a convenient moment.

- A baby has to learn to control its bladder during the first years of its life.

- Urine is around 96% water. The darker the colour of urine, the less water it contains.

- If you eat beetroot or rhubarb, your urine may appear red.

THE PROSTATE

- The prostate gland is a single, doughnut-shaped gland. It is situated below the bladder and surrounding the upper 3 cm (1 in) of the urethra.

- The prostate gland is made of gland, muscle and fibrous tissue.

- It is about the size of a walnut.

- An enlarged prostate may block the urethra. This condition is common in elderly men.

- The prostate secretes fluid, known as prostatic fluid, into the urethra through hundreds of tiny openings.

- Prostatic fluid, together with sperm and fluid from the seminal vesicles, forms semen.

- The prostate is small at birth, but enlarges during puberty.

DRUGS AND THE KIDNEYS

- Some antibiotics are excreted via the kidneys. This is useful as it helps to combat urine infections.

- The kidneys work less well with age. The dose of a medicine that is excreted via the kidney may need to be lowered if the person is older.

- A diuretic is a drug that rids the body of excess fluid by increasing the output of urine by the kidneys.

- Diuretics are used to treat kidney disease, heart failure and high blood pressure. Alcohol and coffee are both diuretics

CIRCULATION AND THE HEART

BLOOD CIRCULATION

- The circulation of blood was first described by British scientist William Harvey in 1628.

- When the body is resting, only 4% of blood is in the heart, the rest is circulating in blood vessels.

- Approximately 13% of blood in circulation is in the brain.

- The blood circulates at a rate of about 5 litres (8.8 pints) per minute when the body is at rest.

- The normal adult pulse rate is about 50-100 beats per minute at rest.

- A pulse rate faster than 100 beats per minute in an adult is known as tachycardia.

- A pulse rate slower than 50 beats per minute in an adult is known as bradycardia.

- Exercise, too much coffee (caffeine), stress or a fever can all cause the heartbeat to increase.

VEINS AND ARTERIES

Artery structure

Arteries have thick, muscular, elastic walls that can resist the wave of high-pressure blood that is pumped with each heartbeat.

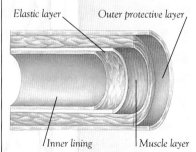

Elastic layer   *Outer protective layer*

Inner lining   *Muscle layer*

Vein structure

Veins have thin walls that enable them to hold large volumes of blood when the body is at rest. Large veins contain one-way valves to stop blood from flowing the wrong way.

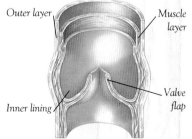

Outer layer   *Muscle layer*

Inner lining   *Valve flap*

INVESTIGATING THE HEART AND BLOOD

- An electrocardiogram (ECG) measures the electrical activity in the heart and can detect changes in rhythm or damage to the heart muscle.

- Exercise ECG testing is carried out to see how well the heart functions during exercise.

- An ambulatory ECG records any abnormal rhythms within a 24-hour period.

- A sphygmomanometer measures the pressure of blood flowing through the arteries. This is commonly known as blood pressure.

- An echocardiogram is a device that uses ultrasound waves to look at the inside of your heart, including the heart valves.

- A chest X-ray shows the position and size of the heart in your chest.

- Cardiac electrophysiological studies record the electrical activity at different sites in your heart using a catheter that has an electrode at its tip.

- A coronary angiogram shows the blood supply to your heart by injecting a special dye through a fine catheter and taking X-ray pictures.

EFFECTS OF EXERCISE

- During exercise, your heart and muscles need an increased blood flow.

- Exercise increases your heart rate.

- The amount of blood pumped out of the heart increases to around 35 litres (61.6 pints) per minute.

- Your blood pressure increases during exercise, but regular exercise will lower your blood pressure while you are at rest.

- As you warm up, the blood flow to your skin increases to help you to cool down.

- The blood flow to your brain remains unchanged.

TYPES OF HAIR

- Terminal hair, such as that in the head, beard, eyebrows and pubic areas is coarse and thick.

- Vellus hair, such as the hair that covers a woman's face, is short, fine and downy.

- Black, brown and blonde hair contains varying degrees of black pigment. Red hair contains red pigment. White hair has no pigment.

- Excessive hair growth in a woman is known as hirsutes

- Short, broken hairs, often found near a site of total hair loss are called exclamation hairs.

- Lanugo hair is the soft, fine hair covering a fetus. It disappears by birth, and is therefore only seen in premature babies.

HAIR IN THE SKIN

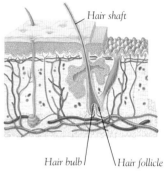

Hair shaft

Hair bulb   *Hair follicle*

SKIN, HAIR AND NAILS STATISTICS

- The thickness of skin can vary from 0.5-3 mm (0.0195-0.117 in).

- There are around 3 million sweat glands in the skin.

- Dust is mainly made up of dead skin cells, which you shed at a rate of around 30,000 per minute.

- The skin weighs between 4-7 kg (8.8-15.4 lb). It is the heaviest organ in the body.

- The average person loses about 80-100 hairs a day.

- A hair on your head may grow for as long as 6 years before it falls out.

- You have around 5 million hairs altogether, around 100,000 of which are on your head.

- Nails grow at around 0.5 mm (0.0195 in) per week. Toenails grow more slowly than finger nails.

Parts of a Nail

The nails on fingers and toes consist mostly of keratin, the tough protein in hair and skin. Nails grow from the matrix, which lies below a fold of skin called the cuticle, and from the lunula, the crescent-shaped area at the base of the nail. The nail plate (the hard, visible part) lies on the nail bed, an area that is rich in tiny blood vessels.

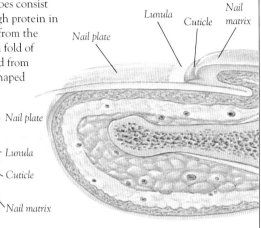

Nail plate
Lunula
Cuticle
Nail matrix

Lunula
Cuticle
Nail matrix
Nail plate

THE EFFECTS OF AGEING

- As a person gets older, their nails tend to grow more quickly.

- Skin becomes less elastic with age. This is why wrinkles develop.

- The effect of gravity on the skin causes it to sag as it gets older.

- Male baldness is hereditary and often starts with thinning at the temples.

- Female baldness develops later than in men and is usually less severe.

- White hair has less melanin producing cells at the base of each hair.

MARKS ON THE SKIN

- Small blisters are known as vesicles.

- Large blisters are known as bullae.

- A patch of reddened skin is described as erythematous.

- Scratch marks on the surface are known as excoriated skin.

- A bruise is called a petechiae. If it is larger than 3 mm (0.117 in) in diameter, it is called an ecchymosis.

- A pupura is a bruise that does not disappear when it is pressed under a glass beaker.

SKIN, HAIR AND NAILS

BONES AND TEETH

BONES

- The femur (thigh bone) is the biggest bone in the body.

- The stapes is the smallest bone in the body. It is found in the inner ear.

- Bones and teeth account for around one-sixth of the total body weight.

- At birth, a baby has about 350 bones, some of which fuse together.

- Adults have 206 bones.

- Contrary to popular belief, men and women have exactly the same number of ribs.

THE SKULL

The skull has several holes in its base through which vital structures connect with the brain. The spinal cord passes through a hole called the foramen magnum, the largest hole. The carotid arteries pass through a pair of smaller holes, called the carotid canals, to supply blood to the brain.

View of the skull from below

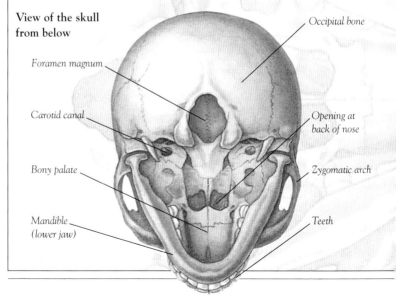

Foramen magnum

Carotid canal

Bony palate

Mandible (lower jaw)

Occipital bone

Opening at back of nose

Zygomatic arch

Teeth

TEETH

- A baby's first teeth start to appear when it is about 6 months old.

- By the age of 5, most children have 20 milk teeth, which later fall out to make room for adult teeth.

- Adults usually have 16 teeth in each of the upper and lower jaws.

- At the front of the mouth, in the upper and lower jaw, there are four incisors for cutting food.

- At either side of the incisors, there is a canine tooth (four in all) which are for piercing the food.

- Behind each canine there are two premolars and three molars, which are designed for grinding food.

- The enamel that covers teeth is the hardest substance in the body.

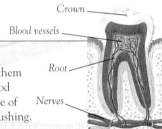

Crown

Blood vessels

Root

Nerves

INSIDE A MOLAR
Molars have up to four roots, which anchor them securely in the jawbone. The nerves and blood vessels pass out through tiny holes in the base of each root. The crown is broad and flat for crushing.

HISTORY OF X-RAYS

- Willhelm Conrad Röntgen, a physics professor at Würzburg, discovered X-rays in 1895.

- They were called 'X'-rays because their exact nature was not fully understood at that time.

- In 1901, Röntgen received the Nobel prize for physics for his pioneering work with X-rays.

- Early X-ray photographs needed to be exposed for up to 30 minutes.

- Such long exposure times caused a number of quite serious side-effects. These included skin burns, hair loss and inflamed skin.

- By 1904, the barium meal had been developed, allowing X-rays to be taken of the stomach and intestines.

- In 1913 William Coolidge invented the X-ray tube. This is the basis of all X-ray machines, including those still in use today.

MUSCLES AND EXERCISE

- An athlete exercising vigorously would need to consume between 3,000-5,000 calories a day.

- Regular, long periods of low-intensity exercise will lead to the production of more energy-providing units, known as mitochondria, in each muscle fibre.

- Regular aerobic exercise increases the blood supply to the muscles.

- More energy units and better blood supply increases your endurance and muscles tire less quickly.

- Short periods of high-intensity exercise, as provided by activities such as weight training, will lead to bigger muscles.

- Big muscles have the same number of muscle fibres, but each fibre is much larger. This is known as hypertrophy.

- Hypertrophied muscles are powerful but tire rapidly as they have little endurance.

- Any changes in the muscles will slowly disappear over several weeks if exercise is stopped.

MUSCLE STRUCTURE

Muscles are made up of tissue that can contract powerfully to move the body, maintain its posture and work the various internal organs, including the heart and blood vessels.

Muscle

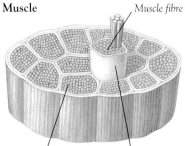

Muscle fibre

Fascicle
Muscle fibres are arranged in bundles called fascicles.

Perimysium
This sheath encloses each fascicle.

Muscle fibres

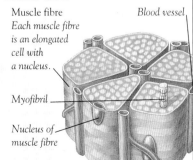

Muscle fibre
Each muscle fibre is an elongated cell with a nucleus.

Blood vessel

Myofibril

Nucleus of
muscle fibre

WARMING UP AND COOLING DOWN

- Warming up before and cooling down after exercise helps to prevent injuries.

- A warm up starts with five minutes of aerobic exercise, such as jogging.

- A recommended series of stretches for all major muscle groups follows.

- Each stretch should be held for at least 10 seconds.

- Avoid bouncing or jerking on the muscle during a stretch, as this may damage or strain it.

- After exercise, repeat the stretches.

ANABOLIC STEROIDS

- Testosterone, a hormone naturally produced in large quantities at puberty, increases muscle mass.

- Anabolic steroids are synthetic hormones that have a similar effect to testosterone.

- Some athletes use anabolic steroids in an attempt to increase their performance. Their use is banned in competitive sports.

- Dangerous side effects include heart attack, diabetes, liver disease and psychiatric problems.

MUSCLE ACTION

Muscles are classified according to their methods of action:

- A flexor muscle closes a joint.

- An extensor muscle opens a joint.

- An abductor moves a body part outwards.

- An adductor moves it in.

- A depressor lowers a body part.

- A levator raises it.

- A constrictor (sphincter) muscle surrounds a hole, closing and opening it.

Weight training can produce bigger and stronger muscles.

BRAIN AND NERVES

MEMORIES

- Declarative memory is based on past experiences. This type of memory includes "general knowledge".

- The short-term memory registers and retains incoming information for a few seconds.

- Remote memories are much more permanent and can persist even after the brain has been severely damaged.

- Semantic memories are those that include facts and concepts, such as the names of famous people.

- Episodic memory includes those events that have been experienced personally, such as a wedding.

- Nondeclarative memory is the memory for skilled behaviours, such as riding a bicycle.

- Nondeclarative memory is stored in parts of the brain called the basal ganglia, the cerebellum and the sensorimotor cortex.

- Retrieving a memory takes the average person about 0.004 seconds.

SPINAL CORD STRUCTURE

At the centre of the spinal cord is a core of grey matter, which contains nerve cell bodies, dendrites and the supporting cells. Surrounding the grey matter is an area of white matter, which contains columns of nerve fibres that carry signals to and from the brain along the length of the spinal cord.

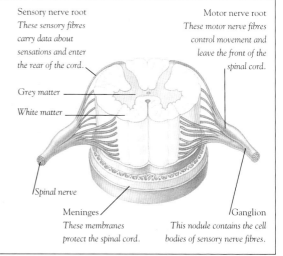

Sensory nerve root
These sensory fibres carry data about sensations and enter the rear of the cord.

Motor nerve root
These motor nerve fibres control movement and leave the front of the spinal cord.

Grey matter

White matter

Spinal nerve

Meninges
These membranes protect the spinal cord.

Ganglion
This nodule contains the cell bodies of sensory nerve fibres.

THE BRAIN STEM

All the nerve fibres from the spinal cord run through the brain stem to the brain, and vice versa. The brain stem contains the following control centres:

- The cardiovascular centre, for the control of the heart.

- The respiratory centre, which controls the rate and level of breathing.

- The swallowing centre.

- The vomiting centre, which can be triggered by poisons or violent motion.

- The eye movement control centre.

- The control of activation – waking up in response to sounds or any other sudden disturbances.

- Control over the orientation of parts of your body in relation to one another and your surroundings.

NERVE STRUCTURE

A nerve consists of hundreds of nerve fibres that are grouped together in bundles called fascicles. The larger fibres are insulated by sausage-like sheaths which are made up of a fatty acid called myelin.

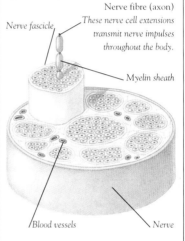

Nerve fascicle

Nerve fibre (axon)
These nerve cell extensions transmit nerve impulses throughout the body.

Myelin sheath

Blood vessels

Nerve

INTELLIGENCE AND PERSONALITY

- Intelligence is a measure of cognition: the mental processes by which knowledge is acquired.

- German psychologist L. Wilhelm Stern was the first to coin the term intelligence quotient (IQ), a figure derived from the ratio of mental age to chronological age.

- The Intelligence Quotient tests verbal, numerical and visual reasoning. It is also used to test the short-term memory.

- Your personality is how you relate to your environment, and how you perceive yourself across a wide range of personal and social contexts.

BREATHING

- There are about 300 million alveoli (balloon-like sacs that pass air into the bloodstream) in an adult.

- At rest, about 4-6 litres (7-10.5 pints) of air enters and leaves the alveoli each minute. This increases by about 20 times during exercise.

- At rest, a normal person breathes about 10-15 times a minute.

- At rest, a normal person moves about 500 ml (0.8 pints) of air in and out of the lungs with each breath.

- A baby takes about 40-50 breaths every minute.

- A substance called surfactant produced by the alveoli cells reduces the surface tension in the alveoli, making it easier to expand the lungs.

AIR PASSAGES IN THE LUNGS

The lungs contain a complex system of air passages. This model shows how the main airway, the trachea or windpipe, divides into the lower airways, known as the bronchi and the bronchioles, before reaching the alveoli.

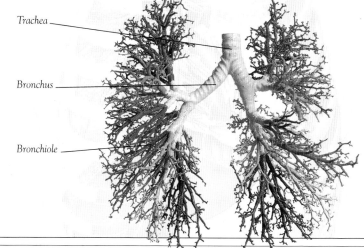

Trachea

Bronchus

Bronchiole

RIBS AND THE CHEST WALL

- Your heart and lungs are situated in a cage-like structure called the thorax.

- The muscles running between the ribs are called intercostal muscles.

- The diaphragm forms the base of the thorax.

- When the diaphragm and intercostal muscles contract, air is drawn through the trachea and into the lungs.

- When the diaphragm and intercostal muscles start to relax, the thorax pushes air out of the lungs.

- The respiratory muscles are controlled by the respiratory centre which is found in the brain stem.

- The respiratory centre is influenced by the level of carbon dioxide in the blood stream.

MAIN AIRWAY

The trachea is the respiratory system's main airway down the throat and into the lungs. Air is treated and filtered in the trachea before it reaches the lungs. Mucus is secreted from the wall of the trachea to moisten the inhaled air. The mucus also traps foreign particles that might otherwise contribute to breathing problems.

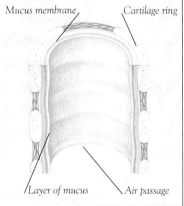

Mucus membrane   *Cartilage ring*

Layer of mucus   *Air passage*

EXAMINING THE RESPIRATORY SYSTEM

- The trachea should be in a central, position. It can be felt between the two collarbones.

- The walls on either side of the chest should move symmetrically.

- Breathing out normally lasts longer than breathing in.

- Normal breath sounds are described as vesicular.

- Tapping the chest to produce a sound is called percussion.

- The tap should produce a hollow sound over the lungs and a dull one over the liver and heart.

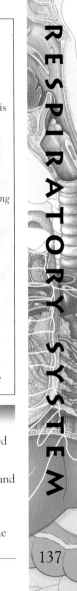

RESPIRATORY SYSTEM

BLOOD

BLOOD AND BLOOD CELLS

- Blood carries oxygen to every living cell in the body.

- It also transports food substances, hormones and waste products.

- It carries warmth around the body and acts as its main defence against disease and infection.

- Oxygen is carried in the red blood cells, which make up about 41% of the blood.

- White blood cells attack viruses and bacteria that enter the body.

- Pus is made up of the remains of white blood cells.

MORE ABOUT BLOOD CELLS

- Red blood cells are produced by the bone marrow in adults and last for about 3 months.

- This production is stimulated by a hormone produced in the kidney, called Erythropoeitin.

- Platelets are small cells that help the blood to clot.

- 4% of the blood is made up of white blood cells and platelets.

Red blood cells outnumber white cells by 500 to 1.

HAEMOGLOBIN

- Haemoglobin is a protein found inside the red blood cells. It boosts the amount of oxygen that the blood can carry by 100 times.

- Haemoglobin contains iron, which it uses to link with oxygen molecules.

- It combines with oxygen when the red blood cells travel through the lungs.

- As the blood travels through the body, it is the haemoglobin that carries and transfers the oxygen to the parts of the body that need it.

- The blood also collects carbon dioxide, which it releases when it reaches the lungs. The cycle then begins again.

- Haemoglobin also acts a pigment that gives red blood cells their colour.

BLOOD GROUPS

Each person's red blood cells have proteins called antigens on their surface, which categorize the blood into various blood groups. Antibodies in the blood are produced against any antigens that are foreign to the red cells. The blood groups are called A, B, AB and O. The ABO system of grouping is important when assessing the compatibility of blood to be used in transfusions. If a recipient's blood contains antibodies to the antigens in the donor blood, a reaction occurs.

Blood group A
This group has A antigens on the surface of the red blood cells and anti-B antibodies in the blood.

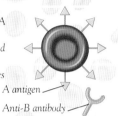

A antigen

Anti-B antibody

Blood group B
People in this group have red blood cells with B antigens, and anti-A antibodies in their blood.

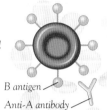

B antigen

Anti-A antibody

Blood group AB
The rarest blood group, AB, has both antigens on the red cells and neither antibody in the blood.

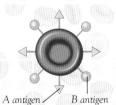

A antigen   B antigen

Blood group O
The most common group, O, has no red cell antigens, and anti-A and anti-B antibodies in the blood.

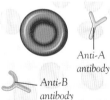

Anti-A antibody

Anti-B antibody

RHESUS BLOOD GROUPS

- Rhesus is another blood group system – blood is either rhesus positive or rhesus negative.

- Rhesus positive blood is the most common type.

- In pregnancy, if a baby is rhesus positive and the mother is not, the mother will make antibodies.

- It is unusual for rhesus antibodies to cause problems in the first pregnancy.

- A second rhesus positive fetus in the same woman may be attacked by rhesus antibodies, and the fetus may die without treatment.

- An antenatal blood test determines the mother's rhesus blood group.

GENETICS

MILESTONES IN GENETICS

- Modern genetics began with Gregor Mendel's experiments on the garden pea, which he reported in 1865.

- In 1869, the Swiss biochemist Friedrich Miescher discovered that nucleic acid occurred in the nucleus of every living cell.

- James Watson and Francis Crick demonstrated the double helix structure of DNA in 1953. They later won the Nobel Prize for their work.

- In the 1980s, it became possible to read the genetic code in DNA and to isolate individual genes.

GENETIC MUTATIONS

When DNA is duplicated, errors may occur that result in a change in a gene. These changes, called mutations, may occur in egg or sperm cells or in body cells, but can only be passed on to a child when they occur in eggs or sperm. Most mutations involve a change in just one unit of DNA, called a base. Mutations may occur spontaneously, as random errors in copying, or may be caused by exposure to UV light, such as that present in sunlight, as well as certain chemicals (mutagens) and radiation.

Normal gene
The sequence of bases in a gene provides the cell with the correct sequence of amino acids that are needed to make a functioning protein.

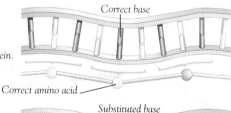

Correct base

Correct amino acid

Mutated gene
If a base in a gene is incorrect, the wrong amino acid sequence may be used to make the new protein. The resulting protein may function poorly or not at all.

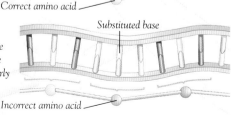

Substituted base

Incorrect amino acid

CHROMOSOMES

- All normal cells have 23 pairs of chromosomes. These are known collectively as the karyotype.

- All except the sex chromosomes are in pairs that are the same size.

Inherited chromosomes determine a child's sex.

- Everybody inherits an X chromosome from his or her mother.

- A male inherits a Y chromosome from his father; females inherit another X chromosome from their father.

- Inheriting an extra chromosome usually proves fatal, except in the case of chromosome 21, which causes Down's Syndrome.

THE HUMAN GENOME PROJECT

- The Human Genome Project was launched in the mid-1980s. Scientists around the world set out to discover a "blueprint" for human life.

- By 2000, it had uncovered the human genome.

- The genetic language is the sequence of bases (the chemicals forming the rungs of the ladder in the double-helix-shaped DNA molecule).

- The human genome is the entire sequence of DNA bases in each of the human chromosomes.

- There are over 3,000,000,000 bases in human DNA.

GENETICS IN PRACTICE

- The sequence of DNA in a hair or sample of body fluid is known as the genetic fingerprint. Forensic experts can match this fingerprint with that of a suspect to solve a crime.

- By examining the DNA of an individual, it is possible to screen for some inherited conditions.

- It may be possible to replace or modify an abnormal gene. This is known as gene therapy.

- Germline gene therapy is the modification of the DNA. This modification can be passed on to succeeding generations. Its use is currently restricted.

141

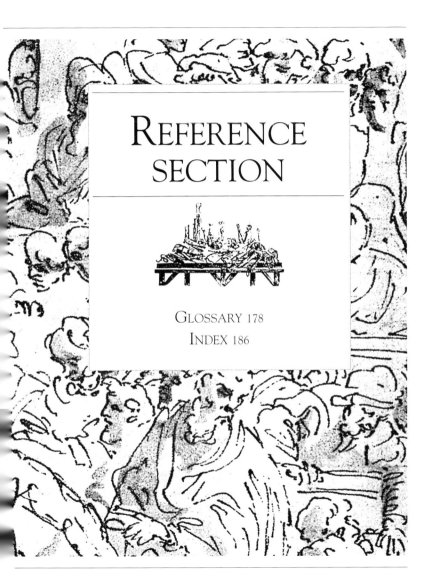

REFERENCE SECTION

LATIN NAMES EXPLAINED

MANY OF THE WORDS that appear in this book are
made up of parts of words, or "roots", that come
from either Greek or Latin. A single word may
have more than one root in it. For example, the
root "hepato" means liver, and "cyt" means cells.
Therefore "hepatocyte" means "a cell in the liver".

HERE ARE SOME MORE ROOTS AND THEIR MEANINGS:

Word root	Meaning	Example
ab	away from	abductor
ad	near, towards	adductor
anti	against, opposed to	antibody
bio	life	antibiotic
brachi	arm	brachial artery
cardi	heart	cardiovascular
cyt	cell	lymphocyte
derm	skin	epidermis
di	two, twice	diploid cell
epi	upon, all over	epithelium
ferent	carrying	efferent neuron
gastro	stomach	gastric juice
gen	a cause of something	antigen
genesis	formation	oogenesis
haemo	blood	haemoglobin
hepato	liver	hepatocyte
homeo	similar	homeostasis
homo	same, identical	homologous
leuco	white	leucocyte
macro	large	macromolecule
meso	in the middle	mesoderm
micro	small	microorganism

Word root	Meaning	Example
mono	one, single	monosaccharide
myo	muscle	myosin
nephro	kidney	nephron
neuro	nerve	neuron
osteo	bone	osteocyte
patho	disease	pathogen
pect	chest	pectoral girdle
pelv	basin	pelvic girdle
peri	near, around	periosteum
phago	to eat	phagocytosis
plasm	living matter	cytoplasm
poly	many	polysaccharide
pulmo	lung	pulmonary artery
ren	kidney	adrenal gland
scler	hard	sclera
tri	three, thrice	triglyceride

SCIENTISTS ALSO USE THESE ROOTS TO DESCRIBE STUDIES INTO SPECIALIZED AREAS OF THE HUMAN BODY:

Anatomy
– The study of the body's structure
Biochemistry
– The study of the chemistry of the body
Biology
– The study of life
Cardiology
– The study of the heart
Dermatology
– The study of the skin
Endochrinology
– The study of the endocrine system
Gastroenterology
– The study of the digestive system
Gynaecology
– The study of the female reproductive system

Haematology
– The study of blood
Histology
– The study of tissues
Immunology
– The study of the immune system
Neurology
– The study of the nervous system
Opthalmology
– The study of the eyes
Osteologist
– The study of bones
Pathology
– The study of disease
Physiology
– The study of the way the body works

NAMING THE BODY

SCIENTISTS AND DOCTORS need precise terms to refer to regions of the body and to show where things are. Here are some important labels they use.

Anterior
Towards the front of the body.

An anterior part of the body is one that lies in front of something else. For instance, the heart is anterior to the backbone. The front surface of the body is called the anterior, or ventral, surface.

Posterior
Towards the back of the body.

A posterior part of the body is one that lies behind something else. For example, a spinous process is posterior to the rest of a vertebra because it projects behind it. The back surface of the body is known as the posterior, or dorsal, surface.

Proximal
At or near the point of attachment.

Many parts of the body, such as the arms, fingers, and nails, are attached at one end. A proximal part is one near the point of attachment, while a distal part is one further away from it.

Proximal

Distal

Anterior

Posterior

Head
The part of the body that houses the brain.

The head houses the brain and many of the body's sense organs. It is protected by the skull, a framework of interlocking bones that surround the brain and support the face. The head is held upright by bones and muscles in the neck. Two special vertebrae at the top of the backbone allow the head to tilt and swivel. The word cephalic describes something in the neck, or the cervix.

Trunk

The central part of the body that houses the heart, lungs, and digestive system.

The trunk is roughly divided into two halves. The thorax, or chest, forms the upper part of the trunk and runs from the base of the neck to the diaphragm. It contains the heart and lungs, which are protected by the ribcage. The thorax can change shape. This movement allows air to fill the lungs. The word thoracic describes anything found in the thorax. The abdomen forms the lower part of the trunk. Most of it lies below the ribcage, and its organs are protected by layers of muscles instead of by bones. The abdomen contains most of the organs of the digestive system, together with other organs such as the kidneys and bladder. The word abdominal describes anything found in the abdomen.

Upper extremity

An arm.

Extremity is the anatomical term for a limb. Each arm contains 30 bones, and is divided into three regions – the upper arm, the lower arm, or forearm, and the hand. The bones meet to form many different joints, including the shoulder, the elbow, the wrist, and the knuckles. Together, these give the arm amazing flexibility. The armpit, or axilla, is found below the point where the arm meets the trunk.

Lower extremity

A leg.

Each leg contains 30 bones, and is divided into three regions – the upper leg, or thigh, the lower leg, and the foot. The joints in the leg include the hip, the knee, and the ankle.

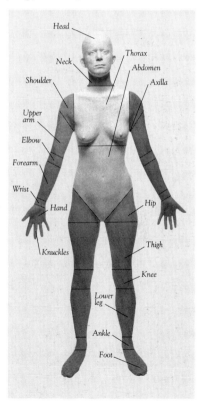

Head
Neck
Thorax
Abdomen
Shoulder
Axilla
Upper arm
Elbow
Forearm
Wrist
Hand
Hip
Knuckles
Thigh
Knee
Lower leg
Ankle
Foot

Axis

An imaginary line that runs down the centre of the body.

The body's axis, or midline, splits it in two. Humans are not exactly symmetrical, so the two halves are slightly different. This is most noticeable inside the body. Many organs, such as the liver, lie to one side, and some paired organs, such as the lungs, are slightly unequal in size. Humans are also asymmetrical from the outside. Many people have one eye or ear higher than the other, and one foot slightly bigger than the other.

Superior

Towards the head, or towards the upper end of the body.

In anatomy, the word superior does not indicate that one thing is better than another. It means that something lies higher up than another part of the body. For example, the adrenal glands are superior to the kidneys. The word superior can also form part of a name. The superior vena cava is a vein that drains blood from the upper body, and the superior rectus muscle is one of the uppermost muscles that swivel the eye.

Inferior

Towards the feet, or towards the lower end of the body.

When used as an anatomical term, the word inferior indicates that one part of the body is lower than another part. For

example, the stomach is inferior to the diaphragm, because the stomach is below it. It is still inferior even if you stand on your head, because all directional terms are taken from a standing position. Like the word superior, the word inferior can also form part of a name. For example, the inferior vena cava is a large vein than drains blood from the lower part of the body.

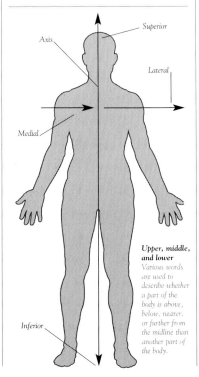

Upper, middle, and lower
Various words are used to describe whether a part of the body is above, below, nearer, or further from the midline than another part of the body.

Cavity
A closed chamber inside the body.

Many of the body's organs are found in closed chambers called cavities. The cranial cavity inside the head contains the brain, while the thoracic cavity contains the heart and lungs. The abdominal cavity contains most of the digestive system. The organs within a cavity often "float" in a thin jacket of fluid. This fluid acts as a shock absorber and enables different organs to slide over each other easily.

Peripheral
At or near the furthest regions of the body.

Something that is peripheral lies away from the centre of the body. The peripheral nervous system, for example, contains nerves that reach to the fingers and toes.

Lateral
Further from the midline.

Something that is lateral lies further from the body's midline.

Medial
At or nearer the midline.

Something that is medial lies near the body's midline.

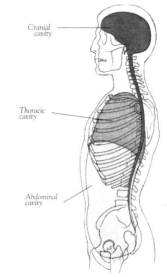

Cranial cavity

Thoracic cavity

Abdominal cavity

Body cavities
There are three major cavities within the body.

Superficial
At or near the surface.

A superficial structure is one close to the outside of the body, or to the outside of an organ. For example, the epidermis is a superficial layer of skin, and the sclera is a superficial layer of the eye. A deep part is one that is located away from the surface of the body. For example, the ribs are deep in relation to the skin of the chest.

THE BODY'S HIERARCHY

LIKE ALL OF THE MATTER in the Universe, the body is
made up of tiny particles called atoms. Collections of
atoms make up molecules, molecules make up
organelles, organelles make up cells, and so on, in a
level-by-level hierarchy (organization) in the body.
When early anatomists studied the whole body, they
were interested mainly in its large structural parts, the
organs. Later, microscopists studied the body at a
different level of its hierarchy – its micro-structural
parts, the cells. Other scientists developed a greater
understanding of the body's functions (what it does).
These scientists were particularly interested in the
nature of body systems and tissues. Only in recent
years, with the development of the electron
microscope, were we able to view the smallest basic
units in the body – organelles and molecules.

1. Body

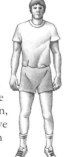

There are more than
six billion human
bodies on Earth. Each
is a unique individual.
But all bodies have the
same basic outer design,
and inside they all have
the same main parts in
the same places.

2. System

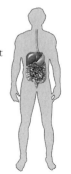

The body can be thought
of as a collection of
systems. Each system
usually has one major
role. For the digestive
system, this is to digest
food so that it can be
absorbed by the body.

3. Organ

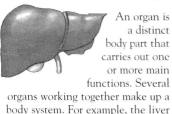

An organ is a distinct body part that carries out one or more main functions. Several organs working together make up a body system. For example, the liver is an organ that is a part of the digestive system.

4. Tissue

Each organ is composed of one or more kinds of tissue. A tissue is a group of similar cells that carry out a specialized job. The liver is mostly made of sheets of hepatocytes – cells that process nutrients.

5. Cell

The cell is the basic unit, or building block, of all living things, plant or animal. A hepatocyte is 0.03 mm (1/900 in) wide and is shaped like a box with rounded corners.

6. Organelle

The cell contains structures called organelles. An important example is the sausage-shaped mitochondrion. Inside it, energy is released from nutrients and made available for the cell's use.

7. Molecule

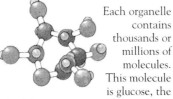

Each organelle contains thousands or millions of molecules. This molecule is glucose, the body's main energy-rich ingredient.

8. Atom

A molecule is a combination of particles known as atoms. A glucose molecule has 24 atoms (including six carbon atoms like the one shown here). All life is based on organic (carbon-containing) molecules.

THE BODY'S INGREDIENTS

THE CHEMICAL SUBSTANCES that make up the human body can be divided into different groups of substances – called nutrients – in the food we eat. The main nutrients in the body are carbohydrates, proteins, lipids (fats and oils), and minerals. If these main nutrients and other substances could be taken from the body and laid out in proportion to each other, they would look something like this:

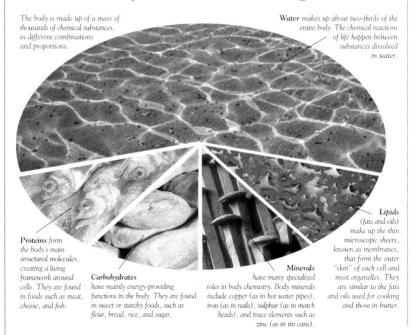

The body is made up of a mass of thousands of chemical substances, in different combinations and proportions.

Water makes up about two-thirds of the entire body. The chemical reactions of life happen between substances dissolved in water.

Proteins form the body's main structural molecules, creating a living framework around cells. They are found in foods such as meat, cheese, and fish.

Carbohydrates have mainly energy-providing functions in the body. They are found in sweet or starchy foods, such as flour, bread, rice, and sugar.

Minerals have many specialized roles in body chemistry. Body minerals include copper (as in hot water pipes), iron (as in nails), sulphur (as in match heads), and trace elements such as zinc (as in tin cans).

Lipids (fats and oils) make up the thin microscopic sheets, known as membranes, that form the outer "skin" of each cell and most organelles. They are similar to the fats and oils used for cooking and those in butter.

WATER IN THE BODY

About two-thirds of your body is water. Two-thirds of this water is inside the body cells (intracellular), where it acts as a solvent containing cell chemicals. It also maintains the shape and size of the cells. The other third of the body's water is outside cells (extracellular).

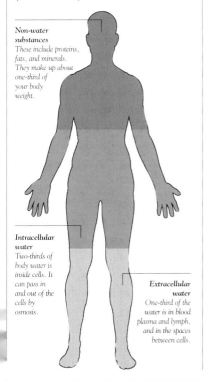

Non-water substances
These include proteins, fats, and minerals. They make up about one-third of your body weight.

Intracellular water
Two-thirds of body water is inside cells. It can pass in and out of the cells by osmosis.

Extracellular water
One-third of the water is in blood plasma and lymph, and in the spaces between cells.

WATER IN AND OUT

Water evaporates from the skin and the lungs. It is also needed to carry dissolved wastes, such as urea, from the body. This lost water must be replaced by water in drinks and food – especially leafy vegetables and juicy fruits. This chart shows the average daily flow of water out of a child's body – although the amounts vary, according to factors such as the surrounding temperature.

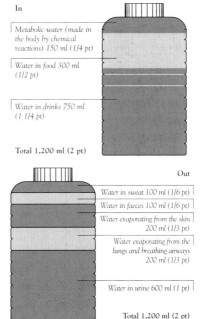

In

Metabolic water (made in the body by chemical reactions) 150 ml (1/4 pt)

Water in food 300 ml (1/2 pt)

Water in drinks 750 ml (1 1/4 pt)

Total 1,200 ml (2 pt)

Out

Water in sweat 100 ml (1/6 pt)
Water in faeces 100 ml (1/6 pt)
Water evaporating from the skin 200 ml (1/3 pt)
Water evaporating from the lungs and breathing airways 200 ml (1/3 pt)
Water in urine 600 ml (1 pt)

Total 1,200 ml (2 pt)

HEALTH AND FITNESS

REGULAR EXERCISE will help to keep you fit and
healthy. People who exercise at least 20–30 minutes
three times per week, lower their risk
of becoming overweight and suffering
from high blood pressure, a stroke, or
coronary heart disease. Ideally, you
should take some form of exercise
every day.

*Heart beats
faster to
pump blood
to muscles*

*Oxygen is needed to
burn fatty acids or glucose
to produce energy*

METABOLIC RATE

The rate at which
your metabolism
burns energy
increases with
exercise. It is
lowest during sleep
and highest during
vigorous exercise,
such as running or
swimming.

*Padded shoes
protect the joints
from impact
damage*

RUNNER

KJ PER HOUR

AT REST	250
STANDING	500
WALKING	750
HOUSEWORK	1,130
JOGGING	2,640
SWIMMING	3,000

PULSE RATE

A pulse is measured by
the number of beats per
minute. If you are fit,
your pulse will stay at
about the rate shown
for your age during 20
minutes of moderate
exercise.

AGE	PULSE RATE
15–19	146
20–24	142
25–29	138
30–34	134
35–39	130
40–44	126
45–49	122
50–54	117
55–59	113
60–64	109

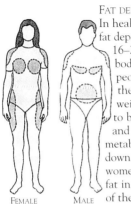

FEMALE   MALE

FAT DEPOSITS
In healthy people, fat deposits make up 16–25 per cent of body weight. As people get older, they often put on weight; they tend to be less active and their metabolism slows down. Men and women store excess fat in different parts of the body.

AVERAGE ENERGY REQUIREMENTS	
SEX: AGE OF SUBJECT	KJ/DAY
Infant: 9–12 months	4,200
Child: 8 years	8,770
Boy: 15 years	12,560
Girl: 15 years	9,560
Inactive woman	7,950
Active woman	9,000
Breast-feeding woman	11,250
Inactive man	10,460
Active man	12,560

BURNING ENERGY

Basketball
Male: 2,430 kJ per hour
Female: 2,080 kJ per hour

Judo
Male: 3,420 kJ per hour
Female: 2,950 kJ per hour

Panting helps take in more oxygen

Running
Male: 3,400 kJ per hour
Female: 2,900 kJ per hour

Exercise produces heat

CONVERSION KEY
4.2 KJ = 1 KCAL

BURNING KILOJOULES
Energy is measured in kilojoules (kJ) or kilocalories (kcal). If the energy you obtain from food is greater than the amount your body burns each day, you will put on weight.

NUTRITION AND DIET

FOR GOOD HEALTH, people need a regular supply of water and nutritious food. A balanced diet provides just the right amount of energy to fuel the muscles and bodily processes, such as tissue growth, breathing, and heartbeat. Many diseases are linked to poor diet. Eating too much fat, for example, can cause the arteries to clog up, leading to heart disease.

VITAL FOOD COMPONENTS

BALANCED DIET
Although most people obtain enough protein from their food, they tend not to eat enough starchy carbohydrates, fibre, vegetables, and fruit. Most people need to eat less fats and sugars. Multi-nutrient supplements containing vitamins and minerals are a popular way to correct imbalances.

VITAMINS
Found in fruit and vegetables, vitamins promote good health.

MINERALS
Also found in vegetables and fruit, minerals keep bones healthy.

FIBRE
The indigestible part of plant foods is fibre; it regulates bowel movements.

CARBOHYDRATES
In the form of starch and sugar, carbohydrates provide body cells with energy.

FATS AND OILS
Animal fats and plant oils keep nerves and other cells healthy and act as a fuel.

PROTEIN
Fish, meat, cheese, nuts, and beans contain protein, needed for growth and tissue repair.

VITAMINS AND MINERALS

TYPE	MAIN SOURCES	FUNCTIONS
VITAMIN A	Cod-liver and halibut oil; butter; milk; egg yolks; liver; fruit; carrots; green vegetables can be converted in the body into Vitamin A.	Helps tissue growth; maintains healthy eyes and skin; promotes the body's resistance to infection.
VITAMIN B COMPLEX/ FOLIC ACID	Meat; kidneys; yeast extract; fortified cereals; bread; sprouts; cauliflower	Maintains a healthy nervous system, digestion, and metabolism; helps enzymes and hormones to function; produces energy; keeps skin and hair healthy.
VITAMIN C	Fresh vegetables; fruit, especially citrus fruit; (Vitamin C can be lost through cooking.)	Keeps skin, teeth, gums, bones, blood vessels, and tissues healthy; improves iron absorption; aids the immune system and heals wounds.
VITAMIN D	Oily fish; cod-liver oil; egg yolks; margarine; butter; whole (fortified) milk; manufactured in skin on exposure to sunlight.	Vital for the absorption of calcium and phosphate from the intestines; calcium is vital for strong bones and teeth.
VITAMIN E	Wheat germ; oil; avocado pear; nuts; margarine; butter; eggs; wholemeal cereals; seeds; nuts; fish; meat; green leafy vegetables	Preserves body fats; helps in the formation of red blood cells; maintains healthy cell membranes.
IRON (MINERAL)	Red meat, kidneys; bread; beans; flour; egg yolk; dried fruit; curry powder; nuts; some vegetables	Essential for the production of the red blood pigment, haemoglobin; fortifies muscles; fights infection.
CALCIUM (MINERAL)	Dairy products; fish; tinned sardines; bread; green vegetables	Maintains healthy bones and teeth; aids muscle contraction; helps conduct nerve signals; assists blood clotting.

INFECTIOUS DISEASES

THE HUMAN BODY may look like a perfect machine, but things can go wrong. This table lists important diseases that are caused by infectious organisms, such as bacteria and viruses, and how they affect the body. Many can be easily caught from an infected person, while others, such as malaria, cannot be spread directly from one person to another.

Amoebic dysentery (Amoebiasis)

Effects: *Multiplies in the large intestine and can cause diarrhoea and bleeding of intestinal wall.*
Transmission: *Spreads through contaminated water and through food, particularly if it is uncooked.*
Causative agent: *Protozoan* (Entamoeba histolytica)

Chickenpox

Effects: *Causes a widespread skin rash that develops into blisters. This common childhood disease is rarer and more serious in adults.*
Transmission: *Spreads through airborne droplets.*
Causative agent: *Virus (Herpesvirus)*

Cholera

Effects: *Causes vomiting and violent diarrhoea. Without treatment, people with this disease can die from dehydration.*
Transmission: *Spreads through contaminated food and water.*
Causative agent: *Bacterium* (Vibrio cholerae)

Common cold

Effects: *Causes inflammation of the nasal sinuses and the mucous membranes lining the throat. It is actually a number of diseases caused by over 200 viruses.*
Transmission: *Spreads through airborne droplets.*
Causative agent: *Virus (Rhinovirus and others)*

Diphtheria

Effects: *Infects the throat and trachea, and, in severe cases, can cause paralysis. In many countries, childhood immunization has made this disease less common.*
Transmission: *Spreads through airborne droplets, or by touch.*
Causative agent: *Bacterium* (Corynebacterium diphtheriae)

German measles (Rubella)

Effects: *Causes a red rash. Usually a mild disease, but it can cause birth defects when it infects pregnant women. Can be prevented by immunization.*
Transmission: *Spreads through airborne droplets.*
Causative agent: *Virus (Togavirus)*

Giardiasis

Effects: *Multiplies in the small intestine, causing internal cramps and severe diarrhoea. It is most common in the tropics.*
Transmission: *Spreads through infected food or water, and through sexual contact.*
Causative agent: *Protozoan (Giardia lamblia)*

Glandular fever

Effects: *Swollen lymph glands, tonsillitis, headache, and lethargy, which may last for several weeks.*
Transmission: *Uncertain, although possibly via saliva.*
Causative agent: *Virus (Herpesvirus)*

Gonorrhea

Effects: *Causes inflammation of the sexual organs. Sometimes spreads to other body parts.*
Transmission: *Spreads through sexual intercourse.*
Causative agent: *Bacterium (Neisseria gonorrhoeae)*

Hepatitis

Effects: *Involves inflammation of the liver. This can cause jaundice (yellowing of the skin) and sometimes severe liver disease.*
Transmission: *Hepatitis A spreads by contaminated food and water, or physical contact. Hepatitis B spreads by infected blood or sexual intercourse.*
Causative agent: *Virus (various types)*

Influenza (Flu)

Effects: *Causes headache, fever, and aching joints. Many strains exist, making it hard to develop immunity.*
Transmission: *Spreads through airborne droplets.*
Causative agent: *Virus (various types)*

Leprosy

Effects: *Infects the peripheral nervous system, causing loss of sensation. This can lead to bodily damage through accidents. It is difficult to cure and is widespread in parts of Africa and Asia.*
Transmission: *Spreads through prolonged close contact.*
Causative agent: *Bacterium (Mycobacterium leprae)*

Malaria

Effects: *Attacks red blood cells and causes repeated bouts of chills and fever. May cause liver and kidney failure.*
Transmission: *Spreads via mosquito bites.*
Causative agent: *Protozoan (Plasmodium species)*

Measles

Effects: *Causes skin rashes and fever. This widespread disease mainly effects children, but can be prevented by immunization.*
Transmission: *Spreads rapidly through airborne droplets.*
Causative agent: *Virus (Paramyxovirus)*

Meningitis

Effects: *Causes inflammation of the meninges (membranes around the brain and spinal cord), leading to headache and fever. Some forms of bacterial meningitis can be very dangerous and may cause brain damage or death.*
Transmission: *Causative agents are often present in healthy people, but only cause disease when they are able to reach the central nervous system.*
Causative agent: *Virus or bacterium (various kinds)*

Mumps

Effects: *Causes swelling of the salivary glands. This disease affects children and adults, but can be prevented by immunization.*
Transmission: *Spreads through airborne droplets.*
Causative agent: *Virus (Paramyxovirus)*

Pneumonia

Effects: *Causes inflammation of the lungs, sometimes making breathing difficult. Pneumonia often accompanies other diseases.*
Transmission: *Usually spreads through airborne droplets.*
Causative agent: *Virus or bacterium (various types)*

Poliolmyelitis (Polio)

Effects: *Range from headache and fever to partial paralysis. This potentially dangerous disease can be prevented by immunization.*
Transmission: *Spreads mainly through contaminated water.*
Causative agent: *Virus (Poliovirus)*

Rabies

Effects: *Fever, delirium, muscle cramps in throat. Immunization given within two days of an animal bite usually prevents rabies.*
Transmission: *Through the bite of an infected animal, such as a dog, fox, or raccoon.*
Causative agent: *Virus (Rhabdovirus)*

Shingles (Herpes zoster)

Effects: *Caused by the same virus that produces chickenpox, and usually affects people over 50. The virus infects nerves. Years after causing chickenpox, it produces a rash on one side of the body.*
Transmission: *Spreads through airborne droplets.*
Causative agent: *Virus (Herpesvirus)*

Smallpox

Effects: *Causes large blisters, or lesions, on the skin, and is often fatal. Once widespread, smallpox has been eradicated*

by a worldwide vaccination programme.
Transmission: *Spreads through airborne droplets.*
Causative agent: *Virus (Poxvirus)*

Syphilis

Effects: *Initially causes sores and rashes. If left untreated, it can lead to organ damage and insanity. It can last for years and may be passed on to children before birth.*
Transmission: *Spreads through sexual contact.*
Causative agent: *Bacterium* (Treponema pallidum)

Tetanus

Effects: *Infects central nervous system, making muscles rigid and later stopping breathing. It can be prevented by immunization.*
Transmission: *Spreads mainly by contact with soil and manure contaminated with bacteria. The bacteria may then enter deep cuts.*
Causative agent: *Bacterium* (Clostridium tetani)

Tuberculosis

Effects: *Infects the lungs and sometimes other organs, causing small lumps called tubercles. Can be treated, but kills many people each year in developing countries.*
Transmission: *Spreads through airborne droplets.*
Causative agent: *Bacterium* (Mycobacterium tuberculosis)

Typhoid fever

Effects: *Causes headaches, fever, and sometimes severe disorders of the digestive system. It is common in countries with poor sanitation.*
Transmission: *Spreads through contaminated food and water.*
Causative agent: *Bacterium* (Salmonella typhi)

Typhus

Effects: *This serious disease can produce fever, blood poisoning, pneumonia, and heart failure. Normally uncommon, it can flare up after natural disasters, when people are crowded together.*
Transmission: *Through the bites of lice, ticks, and other animals.*
Causative agent: *Bacteria-like organisms (Rickettsiae)*

Whooping cough (Pertussis)

Effects: *Causes inflammation of the trachea and airways of lungs, and severe coughing. This disease mainly affects children and can be prevented by immunization.*

Yellow fever

Effects: *Infects lymphatic system and many internal organs. Causes damage to liver and jaundice (yellowing of the skin and eyes). It is widespread in the American and African tropics, but can be prevented by immunization.*
Transmission: *By mosquito bites.*
Causative agent: *Virus (Togavirus)*

NON-INFECTIOUS DISEASES

THIS TABLE lists important diseases and disorders that are not caused by infectious organisms. Some are the result of inheriting defective genes. Others are triggered by environmental factors such as allergens in the air.

Albinism

Effects: *Inability to produce the pigment melanin. People with albinism have pale skin and white hair and are easily sunburned.*
Cause: *Inherited disorder involving defective gene(s).*

Alzheimer's disease

Effects: *Loss of memory, mental confusion, and lack of coordination. Alzheimer's disease usually strikes people over the age of 60 and at present cannot be cured.*
Cause: *Unknown. Possible causes include poisoning by aluminium, and the action of inherited genes.*

Anaemia

Effects: *Deficiency of haemoglobin causes tiredness, a feeling of faintness, pale skin, and shortness of breath. Extreme cases may lead to chronic heart failure.*
Causes: *Several; may be due to lack of iron in the body, inherited abnormalities, the rapid destruction of red blood cells (haemolysis), or the failure of bone marrow to produce sufficient red blood cells.*

Asbestosis

Effects: *Scarring of the lungs, causing difficulty in breathing; can eventually lead to severe disability and death. Asbestosis is one of several lung diseases that are caused by dust or fibres in the air.*
Cause: *Prolonged exposure to fibres of asbestos, a mineral that was formerly used as a building material.*

Asthma

Effects: *Narrowing of bronchioles in the lungs, causing difficulty in breathing. Common in children.*
Cause: *Usually an allergic reaction to substances in the air, or a response to sudden changes in air temperature.*

Cancer

Effects: *Various, depending on the site; may cause a lump under the skin, a non-healing wound, blood in urine, persistent*

abdominal pain, difficulty in swallowing, severe, recurrent headaches, weight loss, tiredness, or loss of appetite and nausea.
Cause: *Various; a cancerous tumour is a collection of abnormal cells that usually form in a specific part of the body (e.g. skin, breast, or lung). They may then spread to the blood and lymphatic systems. The abnormal cells may be due to inherited disorders or exposure to carcinogens (cancer-causing agents) such as tobacco smoke.*

Coeliac disease

Effects: *Damage to the lining of the small intestine, leading to weakness and fatigue. Can be treated with a gluten-free diet.*
Cause: *An allergic reaction to gluten, a protein found in wheat and some cereals.*

Diabetes

Effects: *Abnormally high levels of glucose in the blood, leading to weakness and fatigue, reduced effectiveness of immune system, and sometimes coma. Treated by regular injections of insulin or other drugs and controlled sugar intake.*
Cause: *An inability to produce sufficient quantities of the hormone insulin. This can be triggered by an infection of the pancreas or by genetic factors.*

Down's syndrome

Effects: *Characteristic facial features, including a fold of skin on either side of* the nose that covers the inner corner of each eye; varying degrees of mental handicap.
Cause: *Chromosome abnormality; people with Down's syndrome have three copies of chromosome 21, instead of the normal two.*

Eczema

Effects: *Skin inflammation, often resulting in sore patches and dry, scaly skin.*
Cause: *Several, including allergies, irritation produced by contact with chemicals, and the action of inherited genes.*

Emphysema

Effects: *Damage to the walls of the alveoli in the lungs. This, in turn, leads to breathlessness, and to complications caused by insufficient oxygen in the blood.*
Cause: *Smoking, and, in rare cases, the action of inherited genes.*

Epilepsy

Effects: *These vary from short-lived loss of consciousness and seizures, to temporary paralysis of the whole body. On recovering, the sufferer is often unaware of what has occurred.*
Cause: *Disorders in the normal activity of the brain. These may be produced by infections, by drugs, or by the action of inherited genes.*

Haemophilia
Effects: *Various; severe bruising, sudden painful swelling of muscles and joints, prolonged bleeding after an injury, and blood in urine. Without treatment, bleeding of the joints may occur leading to deformity.*
Cause: *Deficiency of a protein (Factor VIII) involved in blood clotting. The disease is hereditary and only affects males.*

Kwashiorkor
Effects: *Slowed growth, enlargement of the liver, flaking skin, and weakness. Kwashiorkor mainly affects young children, usually when they start to eat solid food. It is common in parts of the world where there are severe food shortages.*
Cause: *Malnutrition.*

Leukaemia
Effects: *Leukaemia is a form of cancer. It can reduce the body's ability to fight infections, and causes tiredness and bruising of the skin. Often affects children.*
Cause: *Uncertain; involves rapid multiplication of white blood cells in the bone marrow.*

Migraine
Effects: *Severe headache, often with vomiting and sensitivity to light.*
Cause: *Uncertain; may be inherited, but is often triggered by particular types of food, and by environmental factors, such as bright lights and loud noise.*

Motor neurone disease
Effects: *Triggers the breakdown of motor neurones in the brain and spinal cord, which leads to gradual loss of movement. Mainly affects people over 50 and is more common in men than women.*
Cause: *Unknown, but most forms of the disease seem to be inherited.*

Multiple sclerosis (MS)
Effects: *Gradual destruction of areas of myelin in the brain and spinal cord. This produces numbness, weakness, and loss of muscle control. MS usually affects young adults and can persist through life.*
Cause: *Unknown, but probably involves an immune system disorder, in which the body attacks its own nervous tissue.*

Muscular dystrophy
Effects: *Gradual breakdown of muscle fibres, causing weakness and sometimes an inability to move around. There are several forms of muscular dystrophy; those triggered by sex-linked genes occur only in males.*
Cause: *Action of inherited genes.*

Osteoporosis
Effects: *Loss of bone density as a result of an imbalance between natural breakdown and replacement of bone. May lead to a gradual loss of height and a rounding of the back. Bone fractures may occur after a minor accident.*
Cause: *Decline in production of sex hormones at a later age can cause the*

decline of bone tissue to accelerate. More common in females, as well as people who are thin and do little exercise. May also be hereditary.

Parkinson's disease

Effects: *In this disease, some of the brain's cells degenerate. This affects muscle control, causing tremor (shaky movement), stiffness, and weakness. Mainly affects people over 60 years of age.*
Cause: *Unknown*

Phenylketonuria (PKU)

Effects: *Prevents the body from breaking down the amino acid phenylalanine in the normal way. If this amino acid is allowed to build up, it can produce epilepsy and mental disorders.*
Cause: *Inherited disorder involving a single defective gene.*

Psoriasis

Effects: *Inflammation of the skin, with rapid division of the cells just beneath the surface. This may produce red spots or larger scaly patches. In severe cases, it is accompanied by arthritis.*
Cause: *Unknown, but in many cases it is an inherited disorder. It usually occurs in sudden attacks caused by illness or stress.*

Schizophrenia

Effects: *Schizophrenia means "split mind". It affects the central nervous system, particularly in young adults. People who suffer from schizophrenia often have a severe emotional disturbance and may behave illogically.*
Cause: *Uncertain. Can be inherited; may also be caused by brain damage or the action of some drugs.*

Sciatica

Effects: *Pain extending down the leg, muscle weakness.*
Cause: *Pressure on the sciatic nerve, usually from a prolapsed intervertebral disc.*

Sickle cell anaemia

Effects: *Red blood cells develop a sickle (crescent) shape, which reduces their ability to carry oxygen around the body. This disease can produce fatigue and may damage internal organs.*
Cause: *An inherited gene that produces abnormal haemoglobin.*

Spina bifida

Effects: *Spina bifida means "spine divided in two". In this disorder, a fetus' spinal cord fails to develop normally and is not completely enclosed within the backbone. In serious cases, it produces a permanent handicap.*
Cause: *Unknown.*

Tinnitus

Effects: *Persistent whistling or ringing sound in the ear that is not produced by real sound waves.*
Cause: *Damage to the acoustic nerve.*

HUMAN BODY TIMELINE

THE STUDY OF THE HUMAN BODY fascinated the ancient world, but from about AD 300, for over 1,000 years, the Christian church discouraged research in Europe. Advances were confined to Asia and Arabia, until the Renaissance gave rise to a new spirit of enquiry.

C.28,000 BC		C.100 BC
C.8,000 BC–C.2,000 BC	C.1,000 BC–C.300 BC	C.300 BC–C.100 BC

C.8,000 BC–C.2,000 BC

• c.28,000 BC Prehistoric sculptures and cave paintings depict the shape of the human body.

• c.6,500 BC Trepanning practised – making holes in the skull is perhaps a form of early surgery.

• 2,300 BC *Nei Ching* (Medicine of the Yellow Emperor) is written in China. It includes a description of the circulation of the blood.

TREPANNED SKULL, C. 6,500 BC

• c.3,000–1,600 BC Egyptians develop interest in anatomy. They believe the heart is the centre of thought and the soul.

• c.2,000 BC Early methods of birth control show some knowledge of human biology;

C.1,000 BC–C.300 BC

sheaths stop sperm from entering a woman's body.

• c.1,000 BC Surgery practised in India, including amputations, skin grafts, and the removal of cataracts.

• c.400 BC Hippocrates (c.460–377 BC), the most celebrated physician of ancient times, describes diseases and their cures. He also draws up the Hippocratic oath – a code of practice for doctors.

• c.384–322 BC Aristotle of Greece makes the first recorded attempts to study anatomy, but he does not dissect a human body.

• c.335–280 BC Herophilus

HIPPOCRATES C.400 BC

C.300 BC–C.100 BC

dissects bodies and claims the brain is the centre of the nervous system.

• c.300 BC Egyptian Erasistratus (310–250 BC) makes many discoveries: the function of the epiglottis in the larynx; the tricuspid heart valve; motor and sensory nerves; and how muscles shorten to pull bones. Incorrectly believes arteries contain air.

• c.300 BC Chinese physician Hua T'o pioneers the use of anaesthesia and performs abdominal surgery.

• c.100 BC Roman physicians practise Caesarian section, a surgical operation to deliver a baby through the mother's abdomen. (A practice still popular today.)

c.170–c.1590 | 1615–1665 | 1672–1691

• c.170 The Greek physician Claudius Galen (129–199) writes *On the Use of the Parts of the Human Body*. He observes that arteries contain blood, not air. Incorrectly asserts that four humours (fluids) circulate through the body to determine a person's well-being. (This is widely believed for the next 1400 years.)

• 1000 Arabian anatomist Avicenna's *Canon of Medicine* is published – his information derives from dissected human bodies.

• c.1450 Invention of the printing press spreads knowledge and coincides with the Renaissance, a period of renewed scientific enquiry.

• 1543 Using stolen corpses as his models, Belgian Andreas Vesalius (1514–64) draws the first accurate anatomical drawings in *De Humani Corporis Fabrica* ("On the Fabric of the Human Body").

• c.1590 Dutch spectacle-maker Hans Jenssen

DRAWING BY VESALIUS, 1543

invents the compound microscope.

• 1615 Italian physician Sanctorius (1561–1636) invents the thermometer, the first accurate method of measuring body temperature.

• 1628 William Harvey (1578–1657), physician to King James I and Charles I of England, describes the circulation of the blood.

BLOOD CIRCULATION, 1628

• 1658 Dutch anatomist Jan Swammerdam (1637–80) uses a microscope to observe red blood cells.

• 1660s Italian microscopist Marcello Malpighi (1628–94) discovers filtering units in the kidneys and the bronchial tree in the lungs.

• 1664 Danish microscopist Niels Stensen (1638–86) recognizes that muscles are made up of bundles of fibres.

• 1665 Physicist Robert Hooke (1635–1703) coins the word "cell" in his book

Micrographia, after studying the structure of a piece of cork under a homemade microscope.

• 1672 Dutch physician Regnier de Graaf (1641–73) describes the female reproductive system in detail for the first time.

• c.1675 English chemist, John Mayhow's (1640–79) chemical investigations on breathing show that a vital ingredient in air supports life. (Later French scientist, A.L. Lavoisier (1743–94) identifies this ingredient as oxygen.)

• 1677 Dutch biologist Anton Leeuwenhoek (1632–1723) identifies male sperm cells.

• 1691 English physician Clopton Havers (1650–1701) observes the complex structure of compact bone.

MICROSCOPE, 1660s

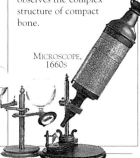

1791   1898

1791–1818	1844–1865	1880–1898

1791–1818

• 1791 Italian anatomist Luigi Galvani (1737–98) discovers that electricity can be produced by chemicals in the body. He touches the legs of a dead frog with two different metals and they twitch.

• 1796 English physician Edward Jenner (1749–1823) discovers the principles of vaccination and immunity. He protects a boy against smallpox by immunizing him with a mild cowpox virus.

• 1800 Italian physicist Alessandro Volta (1745–1827) describes the effects of electricity on muscles.

• 1801 English physiologist Thomas Young (1773–1829) suggests that the eye sees colours – red, blue, and yellow – by responding to three different wavelengths.

• 1816 French doctor René Laënnec (1781–1826) uses the first stethoscope – a rolled-up newspaper – to listen to a patient's heart.

• 1818 The first blood transfusion is carried out by

STETHOSCOPE, C.1820

1844–1865

Dr James Blundell. (Since the four blood groups are not discovered until 1910, it is not very successful.)

• 1844 Laughing gas (nitrous oxide) is used as an anaesthetic during the extraction of a tooth by an American dentist, H. Wells.

• 1846 American dentist William Morton (1819–68) pioneers ether as a general anaesthetic.

• 1851 The ophthalmoscope is invented in Germany to examine the back of the eyes.

• 1853 The first hypodermic syringe is used to give an injection under the skin.

•

CARBOLIC STEAM SPRAY, 1860

1860 English surgeon Joseph Lister (1827–1912) uses antiseptic (weak carbolic acid) to prevent infection during operations.

• 1865 French chemist Louis Pasteur (1822–95) invents "pasturization" to heat-treat

1880–1898

EARLY SPHYGMOMANOMETER, 1883

food, killing off bacteria. He shows how bacteria spreads disease.

• 1880 Czech Samuel Von Basch (1837–1905) invents the sphygmomanometer, the first instrument for measuring blood pressure.

• c.1885 German Rudolf Virchow (1821–1902) recognizes cells make up all body tissues and that many diseases are caused by changes in the cells.

• 1895 German physicist Wilhelm Röentgen (1845–1923) discovers X-rays. First pictures feature his wife's hand.

• 1895 Austrian doctor Sigmund Freud (1856–1939) studies the unconscious mind and establishes a method to treat mental illness: psychoanalysis.

• 1898 Italian professor Camillio Golgi (1844–1926) stains cells and shows how certain membranes are stacked together to form an organelle (a Golgi body).

• 1905 British researchers coin the word "hormone" from the Greek word

1905–1950s	1952–1973	1970s–1990s

for "to stir up".

• 1910 Austrian pathologist Dr Karl Landsteiner (1868–1943) discovers the four blood groups: A, B, AB, O.

• 1912 British biochemist Sir Frederick Gowland Hopkins (1861–1947) discovers vitamins.

• 1918 The first brain X-ray is taken.

• 1920 The first EEG machine is developed to record electrical brainwaves.

• 1931 German physicist Ernst Ruska (1906–88) wins the Nobel prize for inventing the electron microscope.

• 1950 The first kidney transplant is performed by a Dr Lawler in Chicago, USA.

• 1950s Birth-control pill is developed. In general use by the 1960s.

• 1952 Jonas Salk (b. 1914) produces a vaccine against polio. (Mass vaccination begins in the mid-1950s.)

• 1953 American biologist James Watson (b. 1928) and English biochemist Francis Crick (b. 1916) discover

that genetic material (DNA) has a double helix (spiral) structure, enabling genes to pass from one generation to another.

• 1953 American surgeon John Gibbon (1903–74) develops the heart–lung machine to pump a patient's blood during open-heart surgery.

DNA, 1953

• 1954 The first internal heart pacemaker is fitted in Stockholm, Sweden.

• 1958 The endoscope, a telescope that looks inside the body, is developed in the USA.

• 1967 South African surgeon Christiaan Barnard (b. 1922) performs the first heart transplant. The patient lives for 18 days.

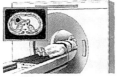

CT SCAN, 1973

• 1973 CT (Computerized Tomography) scan produces a more detailed picture of the internal organs than an X-ray.

• 1970s NMR (Nuclear Magnetic Resonance) scan uses radio waves to produce detailed images of the body's insides.

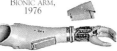

BIONIC ARM, 1976

1976 An electronically operated (bionic) arm is fitted to a road accident victim in Australia.

• 1978 The first test-tube baby, Louise Brown, is born in Britain.

• 1981 The first heart and lung transplant is performed in California.

• 1984 US geneticist John Sanford develops a gene gun, which fires genetic material into a cell at high speed, to alter its structure.

• 1980s–1990s Microsurgery uses advanced technology: fibre-optic endoscopes and lasers.

• 1990s Virtual reality is used to study the body in three-dimensions, and in the field of genetics discoveries are made regularly. The human genetic code is now being mapped.

MEDICAL PIONEERS

THIS TABLE lists the scientists who achieved major breakthroughs in the fields of human anatomy and physiology and medicine.

Addison, Thomas
British doctor (1793-1860)
Investigated the adrenal glands and helped to found the science of endocrinology.

Alcmaeon
Greek doctor and philosopher (born c.535 BC)
Discovered the optic nerve, and realized that the brain – rather than the heart – is the organ involved in feeling, sensations, and thinking.

Alhazen
Arab physicist (c.965-1038)
Studied the physics of light, or optics, and realized that eyes absorb light rays, rather than giving them out, as was previously thought.

Anderson, Elizabeth Garrett
British doctor (1833-1917)
Became the first woman to qualify as a doctor in Britain, breaking the tradition that only men could practise medicine.

An-Nafis, Ibn
Arab doctor and anatomist (died 1288)
First person to show that blood flows through the lungs, forming a circulatory system.

Avicenna, Ibn Sina
Arab philosopher and doctor (980-1037)
Wrote *The Canon of Medicine*, a multi-volume medical textbook that remained in use in Europe for over 500 years.

Baer, Karl von
Estonian embryologist (1792-1876)
Founder of modern embryology. Discovered that a Graafian follicle contains an ovum, and investigated the development of animal form.

Banting, Sir Frederick
Canadian physiologist (1891-1941)
Devised a method of obtaining insulin from the pancreas, providing a way to control the effects of diabetes.

Bartholin, Caspar
Danish anatomist (1585-1629)
In 1611, published *Anatomicae Institutiones Corporis Humani*, or "Anatomical Principles of the Human Body", a major anatomical textbook. His son Thomas Bartholin (1616-1680), who was also a distinguished anatomist, realized that lymph vessels form a separate body system.

Beaumont, William
American surgeon (1785-1853)
Researched the mechanisms behind digestion, working with the help of a man who had been injured in a shooting accident. The injury to the man's stomach allowed Beaumont to collect samples of its contents.

Bell, Sir Charles
British surgeon and neurologist (1774-1842)
Showed that nerves contain many separate fibres (called neurons), and discovered that each fibre carries either sensory or motor signals, but not both. Also deduced that most muscles must be supplied with both sensory and motor fibres.

Benenden, Edouard van
Belgian cytologist (1846-1910)
Discovered that every species, including humans, has a characteristic number of chromosomes in its cells.

Bichat, Marie François
French pathologist (1771-1802)
Showed that organs are made up of different groups of cells, which he named "tissues". Helped to lay the foundations of histology.

Bowman, Sir William
British doctor (1816-92)
Made detailed studies of the fine structure of tissues, particularly in the muscles and the kidneys. Bowman's capsule is named after him.

Broca, Paul
French surgeon (1824-80)
First person to show that particular regions of the brain control specific functions of the body. He realized this after discovering that a man who had been unable to talk had suffered damage to a small part of his brain. Now known as Broca's area, this region controls speech.

Buchner, Eduard
German chemist (1860-1917)
Showed that fermentation could occur outside living cells. This, in turn, led to the understanding of enzymes.

Calmette, Albert
French bacteriologist (1863-1933)
With his associate Camille Guérin, developed a vaccine (BCG) that confers immunity to tuberculosis.

Chain, Sir Ernst Boris
German-British biochemist (1906-79)
Helped to isolate penicillin so that it could be used as a drug.

Chargaff, Erwin
American biochemist (born 1905)
Showed how the four different bases pair up in a DNA molecule.

Chen Chuan
Chinese doctor (died 643)
The first person to have recorded the symptoms of diabetes. During his time, Chinese medicine was more advanced than medicine in the Western world.

Colombo, Matteo
Italian anatomist (1516-59)
Demonstrated that blood flows from the heart to the lungs, and then back again.

Crick, Francis
British biochemist (born 1916)
With the American biochemist James Watson, built a model that showed the double helix shape of the DNA molecule for the first time. This was one of the most important discoveries in modern science.

Doisy, Edward
American biochemist (1893-1986)
Isolated vitamin K, which plays a part in the clotting of blood.

Duve, Christian de
Belgian biochemist (born 1917)
Discovered lysosomes, the organelles that some cells use to digest substances or sometimes themselves.

Einthoven, Willem
Dutch physiologist (1860-1927)
Invented the electrocardiograph (ECG), a device for monitoring the activity of the heart.

Empedocles
Greek doctor and philosopher (died c.430 BC)
One of the first people to realize that the heart is at the centre of a system of blood vessels. At this time, the idea of circulation was still unknown.

Eustachio, Bartolommeo
Italian anatomist (1524-74)
Studied the structure of several organs and systems, including the kidney, the ear, and the sympathetic nervous system. First person to describe Eustachian tubes.

Fallopio, Gabriello (Fallopius)
Italian anatomist (1523-62)
Discovered the tubes that connect the ovaries with the uterus (Fallopian tubes).

Fleming, Sir Alexander
British microbiologist (1881-1955)
While working with bacteria, noticed that a particular mould seemed to kill them. This led to the discovery of penicillin, the first antibiotic.

Florey, Sir Howard
Australian pathologist (1898-1968)
Helped to isolate the antibiotic penicillin, so that it could be used as a drug.

Fracastoro, Girolamo
Italian doctor (1478-1553)
In 1546, published *De Contagione et Contagiosis Morbis*, or "On Cantagion and Contagious Diseases", an early attempt to explain how infectious diseases are spread.

Franklin, Rosalind
British biochemist (1920-58)
Used X-rays to investigate the shape of

DNA molecules. Her research helped reveal its double helix structure.

Galen, Claudius (Galenus)
Greek anatomist (129-58)
Investigated the structure and function of the human body. His ideas – some of them mistaken – stayed in use throughout Europe for many centuries.

Galvani, Luigi
Italian anatomist (1737-98)
Accidentally discovered that electricity can make a muscle contract.

Hales, Stephen
British physiologist and chemist (1677-1761)
Became the first person to measure blood pressure, using a horse. Also measured blood flow and showed that capillaries can change shape by constricting (becoming narrower).

Haller, Albrecht von
Swiss physiologist (1708-77)
Helped to found the science of neurology, showing that nerves carry sensory information to the brain.

Harvey, William
British doctor (1578-1657)
Published *De Motus Cordis*, or "On the Movement of the Heart", the first full account of how blood circulates through the body. He correctly concluded that blood must pass from arteries to veins, although he did not know of the capillaries that make it possible.

Henle, Friedrich
German anatomist (1809-85)
Studied contagious diseases and also helped to establish the science of histology. The loop of Henle, found in nephrons in the kidney, is named after him.

Hippocrates
Greek doctor (c.460-377 BC)
Founder of the science of medicine, which relies on informed diagnosis, rather than myth and magic.

Hodgkin, Dorothy
British biochemist (born 1910)
Developed a technique for investigating the structure of molecules by firing X-rays at pure crystals. She used this to work out the structure of penicillin and vitamin B_{12}.

Hooke, Robert
English physicist and microscopist (1635-1703)
First person to identify cells. In 1665, published *Micrographia*, an illustrated survey of objects seen under the microscope.

Hopkins, Frederick Gowland
British biochemist (1861-1947)
Carried out wide-ranging experiments into the effects of vitamins and showed that they are an essential part of the diet.

Hunter, John
British surgeon and anatomist (1728-93)
Made advances in the surgical treatment of wounds and published one of the earliest works on sexually transmitted diseases.

Khorana, Har Gobind
Indian-American biochemist (born 1922)
Helped to crack the genetic code by identifying which amino acid is specified by all the possible codons (combinations of three nucleic acid bases).

Kitasato, Shibasaburo
Japanese bacteriologist (1852-1931)
One of the discoverers of the plague bacterium *Pasteurella pestis* in 1894.

Koch, Robert
German bacteriologist (1843-1910)
While studying anthrax, a disease found in cattle and people, became the first person to prove that bacteria can cause disease. He also discovered the bacterium that produces tuberculosis.

Krebs, Hans
German biochemist (1900-81)
Discovered the sequence of chemical reactions (Krebs cycle) in aerobic respiration that breaks down glucose to release energy.

Kühne, Wilhelm
German physiologist (1837-1900)
First person to use the term enzyme; discovered that visual pigments undergo a chemical change when exposed to light.

Laennec, René Théophile
French doctor and surgeon (1781-1826)
Studied diseases of the chest and devised the first stethoscope, using a hollow tube and a wooden rod.

Langerhans, Paul
German doctor (1847-88)
Discovered the groups of cells in the pancreas that are known as islets of Langerhans.

Levi-Montalcini, Rita
Italian neurophysiologist (born 1909)
Investigated the way nerves develop, and discovered that many more neurons are produced than are needed. The redundant cells die during development.

Lind, James
British doctor (1716-94)
Found that citrus fruit prevents the deficiency disease scurvy.

Lister, Joseph
British doctor and surgeon (1827-1912)
Introduced the use of antiseptics in surgery. As a result of his work, deaths following amputations were halved.

Lower, Richard
British physiologist (1631-91)
Carried out the first successful blood transfusion using animals, and investigated the function of the heart and lungs. Discovered that blood from veins turns bright red when it comes into contact with air.

Malpighi, Marcello
Italian biologist (1628-94)
Became the first person to see capillaries and investigated other tissues, including nerves and skin. The Malpighian layer in the skin is named after him.

Mechnikov, Ilya
Russian-French bacteriologist (1845-1916)
Discovered phagocytosis in animal cells and found that it is also carried out by white cells in human blood.

Mendel, Gregor
Austrian monk and geneticist (1822-84)
Carried out experiments with plants to show how characteristics are inherited. His research helped to found the science of genetics.

Meselson, Matthew
American biochemist (born 1930)
Investigated how DNA copies itself, or replicates. Meselson showed that each of the two strands in DNA forms a new partner strand, instead of each complete molecule forming a copy of itself.

Meyerhof, Otto
German-American biochemist (1884-1951)
Discovered how lactic acid is formed in muscles.

Monod, Jacques
French biochemist (1910-76)
Discovered a mechanism that controls the way genes are turned on and off.

Montagu, Lady Mary
British writer (1682-1792)
Introduced inoculation against smallpox into England after seeing it successfully carried out in Turkey, where it had been used for several centuries. Mary Montagu had her children successfully inoculated about 50 years before Edward Jenner demonstrated the value of the treatment.

Morgagni, Giovanni
Italian pathologist (1682-1771)
Investigated the causes of diseases by carrying out autopsies, and in 1761, published an important textbook on the subject.

Morgan, Thomas
American geneticist (1866-1945)
Developed the theory that chromosomes carry genetic information.

Müller, Johannes
German physiologist (1801-58)
Pioneer physiologist; investigated the circulation, senses, and nervous system.

Paré, Ambroise
French surgeon (1510-90)
Pioneered the use of dressings in helping wounds to heal, and was the first surgeon to tie severed blood vessels during operations.

Pasteur, Louis
French microbiologist (1822-95)
Pioneer of the science of microbiology; put forward the germ theory of disease, which explains how infectious diseases are caused by microorganisms.

Pauling, Linus
American biochemist (born 1901)
Investigated protein structure and helped to shape ideas about the structure of DNA.

Pavlov, Ivan
Russian physiologist (1849-1936)
Showed that reflexes can be modified or created by learning.

Perutz, Max
Austrian biochemist (born 1914)
Discovered the structure of haemoglobin.

Pinel, Phillipe
French psychiatrist (1745-1826)
Pioneered new methods in the treatment of mental illness. Until his time, patients were chained up in prison-like cells.

Purkinje, Johannes
Czech cell biologist (1787-1869)
Made detailed observations of cells and discovered highly branching neurons in the brain (Purkinje cells).

Ramón y Cajal, Santiago
Spanish physiologist (1852-1934)
Pioneer of the study of nerves, and of nerve staining techniques. He was the first person to suggest that we learn by forming new connections between neurons.

Réamur, René Antoine
French naturalist (1683-1757)
Proved that chemicals were involved in digestion.

Rhazes
Arab doctor (c.865-932)
Prolific writer of medical texts, based in Baghdad. Several of his works were translated into Latin and circulated throughout Europe in medieval times.

Roentgen, Wilhelm
German physicist (1845-1923)
Discovered X-rays, showing their effects when allowed to strike photographic film.

Roux, Pierre
French bacteriologist (1853-1933)
Discovered that bacteria release powerful toxins (poisons) that cause the symptoms of some diseases.

Salk, Jonas
American microbiologist (born 1914)
In 1954, developed the first safe vaccine against polio.

Sanger, Frederick
British biochemist (born 1918)
Became the first person to figure out

the amino acid sequence in a protein.

Schwann, Theodor
German physiologist (1810-82)
Discovered Schwann cells, which surround neurons. Also helped devise the theory that all living things are made of cells.

Semmelweiss, Ignaz
Hungarian doctor (1818-65)
Discovered that personal hygiene, particularly washing hands, had a dramatic effect in reducing puerperal fever, a common disease in childbirth.

Smith, Theobald
American pathologist (1859-1934)
Discovered that a cattle disease could be spread by ticks; this was the first scientific confirmation that infectious diseases could be spread by animals that bite.

Snow, John
British doctor (1813-58)
Discovered the role of contaminated water in the spread of cholera.

Stanley, Wendell
American biochemist (1904-71)
Showed that purified viruses could be crystalized.

Sturtevant, Alfred
American geneticist (1891-1970)
Developed techniques for mapping chromosomes, by identifying genes that are usually inherited together.

Swammerdam, Jan
Dutch microscopist (1637-80)
In 1658, became the first person to observe and describe red blood cells.

Vesalius, Andreas
Belgian anatomist (1514-64)
Published *De Human Corporis*, or "On the Fabric of the Human Body", the first accurate account of the structure of the human body.

Virchow, Rudolph
German cell biologist (1821-1902)
Helped to establish cell theory, which states that all living things are made of cells, and that cells are always produced by other cells. Also helped to lay the foundations of the science of pathology.

Watson, James
American biochemist (born 1928)
With Francis Crick, correctly deduced that DNA has a double helix structure.

Wöhler, Friedrich
German chemist (1800-82)
Showed that urea, an organic compound, could be made from inorganic materials. This disproved the widely held belief that the chemicals in living and non-living things were separate and different.

Yersin, Alexandre
Swiss bacteriologist (1863-1943)
Discovered the plague bacterium (at the same time as Kitasato); made a vaccine to prevent the disease.

GLOSSARY

Abduction
Movement of a body part away from the midline (body axis).

Abscess
A collection of pus cells usually triggered by an infection.

Adduction
Movement of a body part towards the midline.

Alveoli
Tiny air sacs in the lungs.

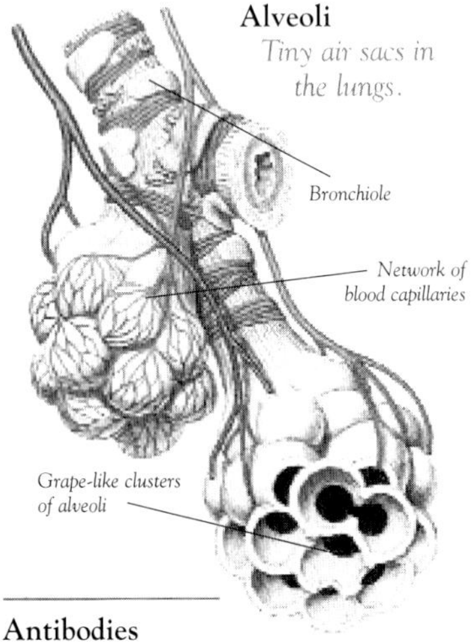
Bronchiole
Network of blood capillaries
Grape-like clusters of alveoli

Antibodies
Proteins, in the blood and other body fluids, that fight infection.

Arteriole
Small artery.

Artery
A thick-walled vessel that carries blood away from the heart.

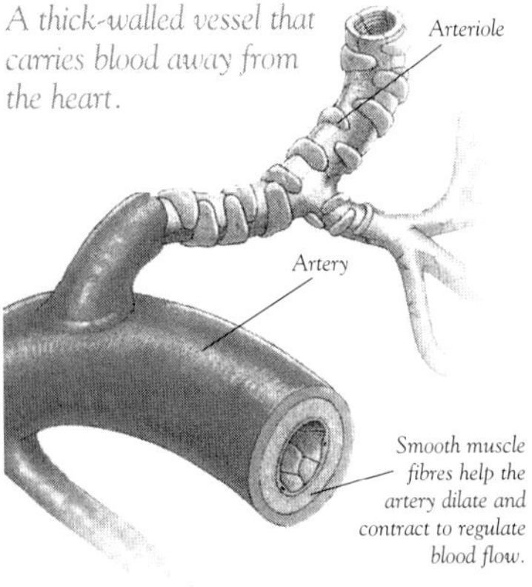
Arteriole
Artery
Smooth muscle fibres help the artery dilate and contract to regulate blood flow.

Arthritis
Inflammation of a joint.

Atria
The two upper chambers of the heart.

Axon
Fine filament that carries impulses away from a nerve cell body.

Bolus
A lump of swallowed food.

Blastocyst
A ball of cells containing a fluid-filled cavity formed from a fertilized egg.

Bronchiole
A small airway in the lung.

Capillaries
Narrow blood vessels that form a network throughout the body.

Cartilage
A tough tissue, associated with bone, that protects joints.

Cerebrospinal fluid
A nourishing and cushioning fluid that surrounds the brain and spinal cord.

Chromosome
One of 46 collections of genes found in a cell nucleus.

Chyme
Semi-digested food found in the stomach.

Cilia
A tiny, hair-like projection from a cell wall, which may have a beating action.

CNS
Central Nervous System (brain and spinal cord).

Collagen
A structural protein found in most body tissues.

Cornea
Transparent layer that protects the front of the eye.

Cortex
Firm, outer part of some organs, glands, hairs, and bones.

Information from a gene is used to make a single protein.

Each chain contains a series of nucleic acid bases that code genetic information.

DNA molecule is made up of two strands.

A chromosome has two identical arms called chromatids.

Cranial nerves
Twelve pairs of nerves that are connected directly to the brain.

Dendrite
Fine projections branching off from a neuron body that receive impulses from neighbouring neurons.

Dentine
Tough layer of tooth beneath the enamel.

Dermis
Inner layer of skin.

Diaphragm
A large, flat muscle that separates the chest and abdominal cavities.

Diastole
Resting phase of the heartbeat.

DNA
Deoxyribonucleic acid – genetic material found in the cell nucleus.

ECG

Electrocardiogram – tracing of electrical activity in the heart.

Stage 1
During diastole (resting), both atria fill with blood. Some blood flows down into the ventricles below.

Stage 2
During atrial systole (pumping), both atria contract, forcing blood down into the ventricles.

Stage 3
During ventricular systole, both ventricles contract, pumping blood out into the body and lungs.

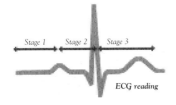

Stage 1   Stage 2   Stage 3

ECG reading

EEG

Electroencephalogram – tracing of electrical activity in the brain.

Embryo

The first eight weeks of life inside the womb when tiny organs are being formed.

4 weeks

5 weeks

8 weeks

Enamel

Tooth coating; it is the hardest substance in the body.

Endocrine gland

A gland that secretes hormones directly into the bloodstream.

Enzyme

A protein that speeds up a chemical reaction.

Epidermis

The outer layer of skin.

Epiglottis

Cartilage flap at top of trachea that prevents food from going down "the wrong way".

Exocrine gland

A gland that secretes its products through a duct into a body cavity or onto the body surface.

Extension

Straightening of a joint, so that the angle between two bones becomes greater.

Faeces

Semi-solid waste products of digestion.

Fetus

The stage of human development, from about eight weeks after fertilization until birth, marked by rapid growth.

8 weeks
The fetus is protected by amniotic fluid and is nourished through the umbilical cord.

12 weeks
The head is large compared with the body. Tiny nails grow. The eyes are closed.

16 weeks
The fetus is covered in fine, downy hair. External genitals are visible. Movements can sometimes be felt from 16 weeks.

Fibrin
Protein involved in blood clotting and wound healing.

Flexion
Bending of a joint, so that the angle between two bones becomes smaller.

Genes
A unit of hereditary information, made up of DNA, that contains enough information to make a specific protein.

Glial cells
Cells that support and nourish neurons.

Grey matter
The part of the brain and spinal cord that contains neuron cell bodies.

Gut
The intestines.

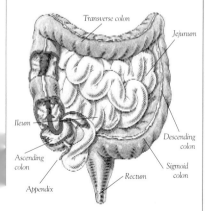

Transverse colon

Jejunum

Ileum

Ascending colon

Appendix

Rectum

Descending colon

Sigmoid colon

Haemoglobin
Red blood pigment that carries oxygen to the tissues.

Hepatocytes
Liver cells.

Hormones
Chemical messengers released from an endocrine gland directly into the bloodstream to trigger an action elsewhere in the body.

Keratin
A tough, protective protein found in the skin, hair, and nails.

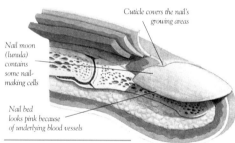

Cuticle covers the nail's growing areas

Nail moon (lunula) contains some nail-making cells

Nail bed looks pink because of underlying blood vessels

Lacteal
Small lymph vessel found in intestinal villi.

Ligaments
Strong, fibrous tissues that bind joints.

Lymph
A fluid that drains from body tissues into lymph vessels – unlike blood, it contains only one type of cell, lymphocytes.

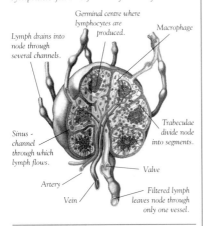

Lymph nodes
Swellings in the lymph system where lymphocytes are stored and through which lymphatic fluid is filtered from infection.

Germinal centre where lymphocytes are produced.

Macrophage

Lymph drains into node through several channels.

Trabeculae divide node into segments.

Sinus - channel through which lymph flows.

Valve

Artery

Vein

Filtered lymph leaves node through only one vessel.

Lymphocytes
Small white blood cells that are involved in antibody production.

Marrow
The soft inner part of long bones, where blood cells are made.

Medulla
Soft, internal portion of some glands, organs, hair, and bones.

Membrane
A thin lining or covering layer.

Meninges
Three membranes that surround the brain

and the spinal cord.

Mitochondrion
Small structure found inside cells where energy-producing chemical reactions take place.

Morul
Ball of cells formed when a fertilized egg starts to divide.

Motor nerves
Nerves that carry signals from the central nervous system to the muscles.

Myofibre
Bundles of cells found in muscle fibre.

Myofibril
Muscle-building blocks made up of two proteins, myosin and actin.

Nephron
Filtration unit found in the kidneys.

Neuron
Nerve cell that can carry electrical impulse.

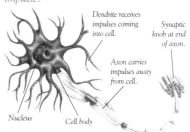

Dendrite receives impulses coming into cell.

Synaptic knob at end of axon.

Axon carries impulses away from cell.

Nucleus

Cell body

Nucleus
The central control region of the cell.

Oesophagus
Tube that leads from the mouth to the stomach.

Organelle
One of many tiny structures found inside body cells.

Osteon
Small unit used to build up compact bone.

Peristalsis
Process by which food is propelled through the digestive tract by waves of muscular contraction.

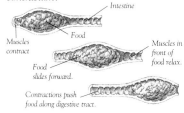

Intestine

Muscles
contract

Food

Muscles in
front of
food relax.

Food
slides forward.

Contractions push
food along digestive tract.

Phagocytosis
Process by which some white blood cells engulf and destroy invading organisms, such as bacteria or a virus.

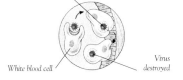

White blood cell engulfs virus.

White blood cell

Virus
destroyed

Pinna
Ear flap.

Pituitary gland
The most important endocrine gland, which is situated at the base of the brain.

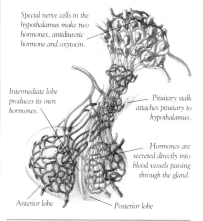

Special nerve cells in the
hypothalamus make two
hormones, antidiuretic
hormone and oxytocin.

Intermediate lobe
produces its own
hormones.

Pituitary stalk
attaches pituitary to
hypothalamus.

Hormones are
secreted directly into
blood vessels passing
through the gland.

Anterior lobe

Posterior lobe

Plasma
The fluid and dissolved substances in which blood cells float.

Platelets
Cell fragments involved in blood clotting.

Pleural membrane
Sheet of tissue lining the inner surface of the chest cavity and the lung's outer surface.

Pulmonary
Relating to the lungs, such as the pulmonary circulation.

Pupil

An opening in the centre of the iris, through which light passes to reach the retina.

Receptors

Specialized structures that detect stimuli and trigger signals that produce a particular response in a body part.

Red blood cells

Cells circulating in the bloodstream that contain haemoglobin.

Retina

Light-sensitive lining at the rear of the eye.

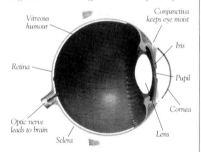

Vitreous humour

Conjunctiva keeps eye moist

Iris

Retina

Pupil

Cornea

Optic nerve leads to brain

Sclera

Lens

Saliva

A digestive fluid secreted by the salivary glands in the mouth.

Sclera

Tough, outer white of the eye.

Sensory nerves

Nerves that carry information from various body receptors back to the central nervous system.

Septum

A dividing wall, such as the nasal septum.

Sinusoids

Blood-filled spaces found in some tissues, such as in the liver.

Superior vena cava

The largest vein in the body.

Sutures

Special joints that lock skull bones together so that they cannot move.

Synapse

Small gap at the junction between two neurons.

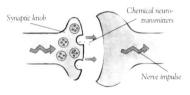

Synaptic knob

Chemical neuro-transmitters

Nerve impulse

Systole

Contraction stage of the heartbeat.

Tendon

Strong connective tissue that attaches muscle to bone.

Thymus

A gland that makes and stores T-lymphocytes in childhood. It almost disappears by adulthood.

Tissue
A collection of cells or fibres that perform a similar function.

Trabeculae
Small bony struts that make up spongy (cancellous) bone.

Tympanum
Eardrum

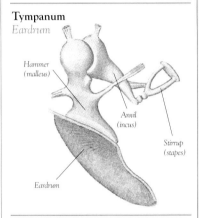

Hammer (malleus)

Anvil (incus)

Stirrup (stapes)

Eardrum

Valves
Flaps of tissue that prevent the backflow of blood in large veins and in the heart.

Open valve

Closed valve

Vein
A thin-walled vessel that carries blood back to the heart.

Ventricles
The two lower chambers of the heart.

Venule
Small vein.

Villi
Small projections in the intestinal wall that absorb nutrients.

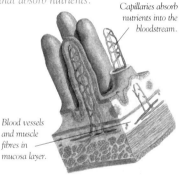

Capillaries absorb nutrients into the bloodstream.

Blood vessels and muscle fibres in mucosa layer.

White blood cells
A variety of colourless blood cells, such as neutrophils and lymphocytes, that protect the body from invading organisms.

White matter
The part of the brain and spinal cord that contains neuron axons.

Zona pellucida
The tough, outer membrane or "shell" of a human egg.

Zygote
A newly fertilized egg.

Index

187

INDEX

Acknowledgements

Dorling Kindersley would like to thank:
Hilary Bird for the index; Louise Cox
and Andrea Jeffrey-Hall for design
assistance; Caroline Potts for picture
research.

Illustrations by:
Joanna Cameron, Mike Courtney,
William Donohue, Simone End, Giuliano
Fornani, Mike Gillah, Nick Hall, Sandie
Hill, Dave Hopkins, Janos Marffy, Kate
Miller, Colin Salmon, Michael Saunders,
Clive Spong, John Temperton, Lydia
Umney, Peter Visscher, John Woodcock,
Dan Wright.

Photographs by:
Geoff Dann, Philip Dowell, Dave King,
Dave Rudkin, Jane Stockman.

Picture Credits
The publisher would like to thank the
following for their kind permission to
reproduce their photographs:

t=top c=centre a=above b=below l=left
r=right.

Allsport: Mike Powell 154l; Lester
Cheeseman: 106tr; Donkin Models:
14–15c; Gorden Models: 56c; Natural
History Museum: 11bc, 11br, 16–17,
18–19, 22–23; Queen Mary's University
Hospital: 169br; Rex Features Ltd: Sipa
37bl; Science Museum: 167br, 168tr,
168–169b; Science Photo Library: 15c,
29tl, 38–39, Michael Abbey 32bl, CNRI
8–9, 15tc, 78–79, 87bl, 89br, Secchi-
Leaque/Roussel-UCLAF / CNRI 15ca,
95cr, Prof C Ferlaud/CNRI 74c, 74cr,
Manfed Kage 58–59, David Leah 104tr,
Dr P Marazzi 66l, Prof P Motta/Dept of
Anatomy, University "La Sapienza",
Rome 20bl, 85tl, 98br, NIBSC 69cr,
OMIKRON 52tr,
David Parker 70l, Petite Format/Nestlè
101tl, D Phillips 92–93, 99tl, Dr Clive
Rocher 77cr, Dept of Clinical Radiology,
Salisbury District Hospital 28bl, David
Scharf 36tl, 64tr, Dr K F R Schiller 85b,
Western Opthalmic Hospital 107tl;
Sporting Pictures (UK) Ltd: 35tl.

Every effort has been made to trace the
copyright holders, and we apologize in
advance for any unintentional omissions.
We would be pleased to insert the
appropriate acknowledgement in any
subsequent edition of this publication.